Teaching Women's and Gender Studies

T0386161

Incorporate Women's and Gender Studies into your middle school classroom using the powerful lesson plans in this book. The authors present seven units organized around four key concepts: Why WGST; Art, Emotion, and Resistance; Diversity, Inclusion, and Representation; and Intersectionality.

With thought questions for activating prior knowledge, teaching notes, reflection questions, reproducibles, and strategies, these units are ready to integrate purposefully into your existing classroom practice. Across various subject areas and interdisciplinary courses, these lessons help to fill a critical gap in the curriculum.

Through affirming, inclusive, and representative projects, this book offers actionable ways to encourage and support young people as they become changemakers for justice.

This book is part of a series on teaching Women's and Gender Studies in the K-12 classroom. We encourage readers to also check out the high school edition.

Kathryn Fishman-Weaver, PhD (she/her) is the executive director of Mizzou Academy. In addition to this book series, she is the author of four additional books in education, *Wholehearted Teaching of Gifted Young Women* (2018); *When Your Child Learns Differently* (2019); *Brain-Based Learning with Gifted Students* (2020); and *Connected Classrooms*, co-authored with Stephanie Walter (2022). She has lectured and led professional development sessions and conferences around the world.

Jill Clingan (she/her) is the composition and literature lead teacher for high school students in Mizzou Academy's Dual Diploma program. This program supports high school students in Brazil who are earning both a Brazilian Ensino Médio diploma from their Brazilian school as well as a U.S. high school diploma from the University of Missouri. At Mizzou Academy, Jill has also authored two high school language arts courses, co-authored an interactive grammar resource, and serves as an administrative editor.

Also Available from Routledge
(www.routledge.com/k-12)

Teaching Women's and Gender Studies:
Classroom Resources on Resistance, Representation,
and Radical Hope (Grades 9–12)
Kathryn Fishman-Weaver, PhD, and Jill Clingan

Gender and Sexuality in the Classroom:
An Educator's Guide
Marni Brown, Baker A. Rogers, Martha Caldwell

The Gender Equation in Schools:
How to Create Fairness and Equity for All Students
Jason Ablin

Let's Get Real, 2nd Edition:
Exploring Race, Class, and Gender
Identities in the Classroom
Martha Caldwell and Oman Frame

10 Perspectives on Equity in Education
Edited by Jimmy Casas, Onica L. Mayers, and Jeffrey Zoul

Wholehearted Teaching of Gifted Young Women:
Cultivating Courage, Connection, and
Self-Care in Schools1st Edition
Kathryn Fishman-Weaver

Brain-Based Learning With Gifted Students:
Lessons From Neuroscience on Cultivating Curiosity,
Metacognition, Empathy, and Brain Plasticity: Grades 3–6
Kathryn Fishman-Weaver

Teaching Women's and Gender Studies

Classroom Resources on Resistance, Representation, and Radical Hope (Grades 6–8)

Kathryn Fishman-Weaver,
and Jill Clingan

Routledge
Taylor & Francis Group

NEW YORK AND LONDON

Cover image: © Getty Images

First published 2023
by Routledge
605 Third Avenue, New York, NY 10158

and by Routledge
4 Park Square, Milton Park, Abingdon, Oxon, OX14 4RN

Routledge is an imprint of the Taylor & Francis Group, an Informa business

© 2023 Kathryn Fishman-Weaver and Jill Clingan

The right of Kathryn Fishman-Weaver, PhD, and Jill Clingan to be identified as authors of this work has been asserted in accordance with sections 77 and 78 of the Copyright, Designs and Patents Act 1988.

All rights reserved. The purchase of this copyright material confers the right on the purchasing institution to photocopy or download pages which bear the copyright line at the bottom of the page. No other parts of this book may be reprinted or reproduced or utilised in any form or by any electronic, mechanical, or other means, now known or hereafter invented, including photocopying and recording, or in any information storage or retrieval system, without permission in writing from the publishers.

Trademark notice: Product or corporate names may be trademarks or registered trademarks, and are used only for identification and explanation without intent to infringe.

ISBN: 978-1-032-26694-7 (hbk)
ISBN: 978-1-032-24661-1 (pbk)
ISBN: 978-1-003-28950-0 (ebk)

DOI: 10.4324/9781003289500

Typeset in Palatino
by Apex CoVantage, LLC

Access the Support Material at www.routledge.com/9781032246611

Contents

Support Material

The handouts in this book are also available on the book product page online, so you can easily print them for classroom use. To access these downloads, go to routledge.com/9781032246611 and click on the "Support Material" link.

Acknowledgments

We are grateful for the young people we work and learn with. Their vision, leadership, and radical hope that the world can be more just, inclusive, and vibrant inspires and fuels our work.

We also want to thank each other. From shared desserts (that crème brûlée in São Paulo), to book recommendations (so much poetry), to service projects addressing food insecurity in mid-Missouri, to eating ice cream with middle school scholars on a school roof in Brazil (dessert again), we are grateful to each other. For all our shared passions, and more important, all our different experiences and perspectives, we both believe the other is the right partner and co-author for this project. We also want to acknowledge our families who believed in and supported this work. The love of our spouses, our children, and our parents is evident throughout this text.

The incredible advisory editors who gifted us their time, expertise, and compassion made this book immeasurably stronger. Dr. Elisa Glick, Dr. Adrian Clifton, Dr. Dena Lane-Bonds, Stefani Domingues, and Lisa DeCastro were gracious in pointing out our blind spots, suggesting new directions, emailing important additions, sending specific notes and corrections, teaching us a better way, and offering their continued encouragement. Each of these remarkable teachers are leaders in their fields and communities. In this book, you will read section forwards and letters from the advisory editors listed above; however, these give you only a glimpse into the significant mark these five thought leaders have left on this text.

An important origin story for this project are the Women's History Month resources we developed each year. As such, we want to thank the colleagues who helped with these teaching guides, especially Brian Stuhlman, Dr. Sherry Denney, Stephanie Walter, Lou Jobst, Anthony Lehman-Plogger, and Nina Sprouse. We are also grateful for Dr. Thitinun "Ta" Boonseng, Artitaya "New" Jantaraprapa, Dr. Shivasankalp "Sankalp" Shivaprakash, Greg Soden, Rachel Andresen, and Dr. Jennifer Fisher who sent notes and resources that broadened our understanding.

Several schools and educators were early champions of these lessons. In particular, we would like to thank Robert "Bert" Garner and Rossella Beer and Luiza Dutra for sharing meaningful ways they implement creative and inclusive practices in their school communities in São Paulo, SP. Additionally, we are grateful to Matheus Nucci Mascarenhas and Marília Mascarenhas for their important contributions to this book.

We are indebted to teachers who were important in our own feminist journeys. Kathryn would like to thank Dr. Barbara Bank (in fond memory); Dr. Christine Patterson; Dr. Brad Wing; and Dr. Joan Hermsen, who first introduced her to feminist scholarship as an undergraduate; and later Dr. Jeni Hart, who supported her work as a feminist researcher during her doctoral program. Jill would like to thank Mrs. Deborah Murray, Dr. Jerry Dees, Dr. Karin Westman, and Dr. Phil Nel, graduate school professors who taught her how much stories matter and who often made her think, as a student in their classes, that there was no place in the world she would rather be.

Finally, thank you (truly, purposefully) to Lauren Davis, Julia Giordano, Emma Capel, and the Routledge team for their belief in this project and for their wisdom and care in bringing it to fruition.

Meet the Authors

Kathryn Fishman-Weaver, PhD (she/her), began her teaching career as a special education teacher in a public K-8 school in Oakland, CA. Since then, she has taught and led programs in special education, gifted education, English language arts, and teacher preparation. Kathryn currently serves as the executive director of Mizzou Academy. She is the author of four additional books in education, *Wholehearted Teaching of Gifted Young Women* (2018); *When Your Child Learns Differently* (2019); *Brain-Based Learning with Gifted Students* (2020); and *Connected Classrooms*, co-authored with Stephanie Walter (2022). Despite these academic publications, her first literary love is poetry, and that is a love that has lasted a lifetime. Kathryn's work has appeared in numerous publications and been referenced by the U.S. Department of Education. In addition to work in K-12 schools, Kathryn also supports the University of Missouri's teacher education program by coordinating required courses on culturally responsive, ethical, and community-engaged teaching practices. She has lectured and led professional development sessions and conferences around the world.

Jill Clingan (she/her) is the composition and literature lead teacher for high school students in Mizzou Academy's Dual Diploma program. This program supports high school students in Brazil who are earning both a Brazilian Ensino Médio diploma from their Brazilian school as well as a U.S. high school diploma from the University of Missouri. At Mizzou Academy, Jill has authored two high school language arts courses, co-authored an interactive grammar resource, and serves as an administrative editor. She has traveled to southeast Brazil to work with schools and lead and present at international educational conferences. Jill holds a bachelor's degree in psychology and a master's degree in English literature. Before teaching at Mizzou Academy, she homeschooled her daughter through much of elementary school and taught writing and literature classes at Kansas State University. Additionally, Jill's work has appeared in *Practicing Families* and *Grit*. If you showed up on the five-acre spot of land where she lives with her family, you might very well find her quoting poetry to her motley crowd of dogs, cats, chickens, turkeys, and ducks.

Introduction

Gender equality is not only a fundamental human right, but a necessary foundation for a peaceful, prosperous and sustainable world.

(United Nations, 2020)

Jill and I (Kathryn) work for a global school system. This work with young people and educators from around the world has informed how we think about feminisms, justice, access, and the inherent reciprocity between global and local perspectives (see pp. 26-27 for more information on global and *transnational feminisms*). The United Nations provides a strong foundation for understanding the global (and multitude of local) landscapes related to gender and justice.

In 2010, UN Women was established to help advance and coordinate this ongoing work from within the United Nations. In 2015, the United Nations released 17 Sustainable Development Goals (SDGs). The United Nations' fifth SDG is to achieve gender equality and to empower all women and girls. There are even deeper roots in the Commission on the Status of Women, which remains the main global intergovernmental body dedicated to women's empowerment and gender justice work. Since its founding in 1946, the Commission on the Status of Women has been able to report on significant accomplishments, yet much more work still needs to be accomplished. According to reports by the United Nations, women and girls continue to have unequal access to resources including basic resources

DOI: 10.4324/9781003289500-1

(e.g. food, shelter), leadership positions, educational opportunities, and safety. For example,

◆ Women and girls are significantly more likely to live in extreme poverty (UN Women, 2021b).
◆ Women hold only 28% of managerial positions (United Nations, n.d.-c) and remain underrepresented at all levels of political leadership (UN Women, 2021a).
◆ Women and girls are paid 23% less than their men counterparts—this figure is compounded for women of color (UN Women, n.d.-a.).
◆ "1 in 5 women and girls between the ages of 15 and 49 report experiencing physical or sexual violence by an intimate partner within a 12-month period" (United Nations, n.d.-a), fewer than 40% of these women and girls seek help, and fewer than 10% report violence to the police (UN Women, 2022).
◆ 129 million girls are not in school, and less than half of primary and secondary schools have achieved gender parity (UNICEF, n.d.).
◆ According to the United Nations (2020) Free and Equal Report, official data on violence against the LGBTQIA+ community is difficult to collect. This is because of a lack of stable systems and legal protections for reporting crimes against LGBTQIA+ individuals. However, all analyses point to a clear pattern of widespread and brutal violence against LGTBTQIA+ individuals, which has been reported in all regions of the world (Free & Equal United Nations for LGBTI Equality, n.d.).

In what ways can the middle school classroom become a site for exploring and even *complicating* these big issues. For example, as we (Kathryn and Jill) consider what feminism and gender justice mean to us, we include issues of racial justice (such as health disparities, racism, and intergenerational trauma) and LGBTQIA+ inclusion (including health disparities, hetereosexism, and gender-based violence) as essential issues for gender justice in the 21st century. In teaching systemic and global issues, how can you and your class communities center humanity and hope? When educators approach global awareness from a people-centered perspective (Fishman-Weaver and Walter, 2022), they move beyond a curriculum of despair and pain (Tuck, 2009) and enter a space that is honest, difficult, and also full of hope, resistance, and joy. In these chapters, we (Kathryn and Jill) celebrate the incredible ways advocates thread knowledge, innovation, and care across all sectors of industry, influence, and humanity. The following teaching units shine a light on leaders, creators, activists, and dreamers who have and are changing the world.

Believing that personal stories are the shortest distance between people, these chapters honor that the cartography of oppression and resistance is as varied as a topographic map. Yet our collective stories, as different as they—as we—are, paint a global landscape of diversity, of beauty, of pain, of courage, and of triumph.

If you scan a university course list, you will likely find classes on Women's and Gender Studies. However, if you scan a middle school or high school course directory, such courses are far less likely. This book offers ideas, strategies, and activities to begin to fill this gap in the field, and you can begin this work within the classes you already teach. Women's and Gender Studies is inherently interdisciplinary in nature. These lessons include meaningful extensions and activities in language arts, social studies, the sciences, and the arts, among others. Recognizing the power of asset-based approaches and knowing that language matters, we (Kathryn and Jill) refer to the K-12 students we work with as *scholars*. The lessons included in the following chapters ask young people to engage in critical analysis; to launch action projects in their local communities; and to participate in the production of knowledge through their writing, advocacy, art, and creative works. Our own experiences with young people have taught us that they are not waiting to become scholars and leaders; instead, they are already pushing the boundaries of learning and impacting change. By choosing to use the term scholars, we (Kathryn and Jill) hope also to open up and expand the definition of what and who counts within the lexicon of scholarship. Is a 16-year-old who creates an art installation on mental health a scholar? Is an 11-year-old who launches a community-wide food drive a scholar? Is a 14-year-old who speaks to their city council about health disparities a scholar? Absolutely. As a feminist project, we do not see scholarship as something that can happen only within a specific higher education context. Instead, throughout this book, we are proud to center and honor the wisdom and scholarship that comes from the lived experiences, passion, and efforts of young people.

In her seminal work on literature, Dr. Rudine Sims Bishop (1990) asserted that scholars need books that serve as windows, mirrors, and sliding glass doors. We believe the same is true across all curricula. Young people need *mirrors* to see themselves, their realities, and their experiences in the people they study. They also need *windows* to meet people, realities, and experiences that are different from their own. And finally, our classrooms need *sliding glass doors* that encourage young people to walk boldly into new realities.

Representative future casting is important for self-efficacy. When young people look into their school curricula, do they find confident and inspiring change makers who share their identities? We (Jill and Kathryn) have written this book with a belief that young people can impact change, lead movements, and create projects that matter. Our hope is that these lessons support you in celebrating scholars not only for who they are right now but also for who they are becoming. We (Kathryn and Jill) believe the classroom can be a powerful site for beginning this work toward justice, inclusion, and representation.

Positionality

As with most big ideas, this project can be traced to several distinct origin moments, including our (Kathryn and Jill's) separate formative and personal experiences of gender discrimination, transformative conversations we've shared with our own daughters *and* sons, and to our curriculum and teaching work in K-12 classrooms. Each of these experiences shaped who we are as feminist educators, influenced the content of this book, and informed our persistence for bringing this text to fruition.

The most palpable inciting incident is the annual series of teaching resources we release each spring for Women's History Month. These classroom activities were our first conversations with each other about what feminist teaching could be in middle and high school spaces. This thought work was important for our professional growth as educators and shaped further dialogue and decisions within our own school community. One year the series helped us launch an author audit of texts in our language arts courses, which was followed by a dramatic increase in women's voices, authors, and scholars in our curriculum. This work then led to a more intersectional approach to curricular work centered on culturally responsive choices about representation and diversity across many different identities (Gay, 2002). In addition to complicating the canon (Illich and Alter Smith, 2018) and offering more diverse worldviews across our courses, we also wanted to "anchor curriculum in the everyday lives of our scholars" (Kozleski, 2010, p. 6).

The annual Women's History Month project became both a celebration and an initiative, what my (Kathryn's) mother called "an agenda for good." Each year we aligned our resources to the National Women's History Month Alliance's annual theme. In January or February, we sent out a call for proposals to our colleagues, and then we poured into the project with resolve to release it as close to March 1 as possible. We challenged the teachers in our communities to think of our Women's History Month resources as seeds that grew well beyond March. Knowing that these seeds would need what one of our colleagues calls "care and feeding," we wanted to give teachers a volume of resources they could integrate throughout the year. And so, aptly, one weekend in March, we decided to look more critically at the resources we had built out over the past several years to see if they might offer a celestial map for something bigger, something more permanent, something much like the book you are holding in your hands.

We (Kathryn and Jill) are career educators, introverts, poetry lovers, and mothers. We can map our friendship from a bookshop in central Missouri; to school events in São Paulo, SP; to deep conversations around my (Kathryn's) kitchen table, preferably with some of Jill's baked goods. We are also both White, cisgender women of European (eastern and western) descent. We recognize that our similar lived experiences limit the scope of this project. Being aware of this limitation, we strive to (1) be transparent about our own positionality; (2) intentionally work with advisors and editors who represent different identities and lived experiences from our own; (3) draw on the work of Black, Latina, Indigenous, Asian, and LGBTQIA+ scholars; and (4) iterate based on the feedback we've received implementing these lessons in global classrooms.

Across these units, we (Kathryn and Jill) are committed to teaching a multiplicity of voices. And yet, even with these commitments, there are some lived experiences that, despite study and friendship, we know we will never fully understand. We recognize that if authors from other backgrounds were writing this text, it would likely be a very different book. One system we've employed to expand the voices and perspectives in this book is working with advisory editors on each conceptual section. These editors gave us important feedback on our chapters, points to consider or clarify, and impressions on how these activities might function in their classrooms. We are grateful to the five advisory editors who each took on a conceptual section as an advisor and thought partner. These editors bring diverse identities and lived experiences to this text. They were critical in helping Jill and me (Kathryn) identify our blind spots and making this text stronger and more effective. Each conceptual chapter includes a forward by the advising editor where they share their thoughts on the concepts and activities.

While we (Jill and Kathryn) share much in common, we also have important differences that influenced the content and structure of this text.

Kathryn Fishman-Weaver (she/her). My grandmothers—the daughters and granddaughters of immigrants—were among my most important teachers. As a young woman, my grandma Sophie wrote for an underground newspaper in Brooklyn, studied languages at night school, and hitchhiked to national protests. Meanwhile, my grandma Norma taught in a one-room schoolhouse in Northwestern Iowa, wrote poetry that she kept mostly to herself, and shared an incredible love story with her high school sweetheart. I am deeply indebted to the strong-willed women in my family including my grandmothers, my mother, my sister, my daughter, my aunts, and soon a daughter-in-law. You can see their influence across so many of my decisions and ways of being.

In high school, I performed original (often angsty) poems in the coffee shop circuit on the main drag of my hometown in middle America. I had a close circle of girlfriends who supported me during my formative years. In college, I minored in Women's and Gender Studies and changed my major several times, finally landing on sociology with an extra minor in English writing. Soon after graduating, my spouse and I ran off to California, where I worked for a social justice nonprofit and then suddenly changed course again to become a schoolteacher for the Oakland Unified School District. The classroom became my home, my scholars my new instructors, and teaching my vocation. Along the way, I earned a master's degree in special education and a PhD in educational leadership and policy analysis. I have now taught nearly every grade from kindergarten through university. I've taught language arts, elementary, high school, special education, gifted education, math, finance, and teacher education. I've facilitated several research studies on gender and education, including student-led projects on the state of feminism, the lived experiences of young women during the transition from high school to college, and how the visual arts can support emotional processing. For the past six years, I've served as a director for a global K-12 school system, which is also where I met Jill.

Jill Clingan (she/her). I grew up with two strong women as my role models—my mom and my grandma—who exemplified strength, resilience, wisdom, grace, and faith. My grandma married her high school sweetheart and then spent the next 64 years deeply loving my grandpa, her children, her grandchildren, and her great grandchildren. She was also famous for her pies, an art I try to emulate. While in many ways she filled what appeared to be a very traditional role as a mom and pastor's wife, she also did not always bend to the norms expected of her, an art I try to emulate as well. My mom was a preschool teacher who prioritized and adored her family. She nurtured me, supported me, and passed on to me her perceptive wisdom. She also fiercely believes in me, and I carry that strength with me. Now, my daughter is part of that circle, and I want to emulate her courage and confidence. I am so very proud of her, and in a twist of parental role reversal that I didn't quite expect, I want her to be proud of me, too.

I did not grow up learning feminist theory, and any feminist writers I read were by pure accident, but I was a voracious reader, and I was always attracted to women authors and books with strong women characters. Louisa May Alcott was my beloved childhood companion, and as I got older, I discovered the works of Virginia Woolf, Sylvia Plath, Alice Walker, Kate Chopin, and Maya Angelou. I had always wanted to be an English teacher, but as a senior in high school, my science teacher stopped me in the hall one day and told me I should reconsider this career path. Her words stunned me and ultimately changed the course of my life. Instead of following my dream to become an English teacher, I pursued a different educational path, but after wrestling with myself for years, I finally followed my heart and went back to school to earn a degree in my first love: English. I taught writing and literature courses at Kansas State University and then took an unexpected detour in my educational and career path as I spent several years homeschooling my daughter. For the past six years, I have been a composition and literature lead teacher for the global K-12 program where I met Kathryn.

Our paths, as different as they are, have organically led us to a space to write this book. Kathryn and I (Jill) have worked on many projects together over the past several years, but we always come around to this space, a space to amplify the voices of women and share their stories, their contributions, their challenges, and their triumphs with teachers and scholars in the classroom. This book is more than a project for us; it is a mission of our hearts and a work of our souls. As such, it is a book that is more than two-dimensional words on a page. It is a living space for us to co-create expansive spaces in our schools, spaces that advance justice and inclusion, celebrate more complete stories, and encourage young people to engage in making the world a more just place right now.

About This Book

This book is informed by feminist scholarship around the production of knowledge, the power of personal narratives, and the intersections of identity. It is deepened by the wisdom gained through collectives. These chapters both acknowledge the ways privilege and power complicate our systems and encourage radical hope that those same systems can be challenged and reimagined. Believing that "feminism is for everybody" (CNN—bell hooks, 2000) and that "we should all be feminists" (Adichie, 2014), this book aims to offer a text that middle school teachers and scholars can see themselves and their communities in. Although we could not include photos of the 100+ key figures celebrated in the following lessons, we do encourage you to share images of the artists, activists, scientists, advocates, writers, and student leaders featured in these lessons. These key figures represent ethnic, racial, religious, gender, cultural, and ability diversity. It is our hope that the units include multiple mirrors and windows for your scholars (Bishop, 1990). Each unit is organized around three core concepts: representation, resistance, and radical hope. These concepts inform how the following chapters were developed, the voices and stories we strove to include, and how we (Jill and Kathryn) imagined agency being negotiated and celebrated in classroom spaces.

The book is structured around the following three key concepts for student inquiry, plus a proseminar on intersectionality.

- ◆ Concept 1: Why WGST?
  - Unit 1: Feminist Theory: Introduction
  - Unit 2: We Can All be Changemakers for Justice
- ◆ Concept 2: Art, Emotion, and Resistance
  - Unit 3: Affective Development: In More Voices
  - Unit 4: Art as Resistance
- ◆ Concept 3: Diversity, Inclusion, and Representation
  - Unit 5: Our Vibrant World: Representation
  - Unit 6: From our Ancestors: Change Movements for a More Just World
- ◆ Proseminar: Intersectionality

Each concept begins with a section overview with learning objectives and guiding questions for both scholars and educators. The concepts include an activity to honor prior knowledge, two units related to the overarching concept, several lessons for exploration, and a synthesis project.

In addition to lesson content, each concept also includes a care letter for educators. Teaching is heart-heavy work. Teaching Women's and Gender Studies often taps into complicated, charged, and sensitive issues that require additional heart work. In these care letters, we (Kathryn and Jill) want you, too, to feel seen and affirmed in all you are carrying by engaging in this important content.

If possible, we recommend starting with Concept 1, which offers a foundation for Women's and Gender Studies and key themes developed throughout the text. The lessons are written in general enough terms to be accessible across the middle school context. As with all lessons, you may find there are ideas, vocabulary, or activities that require more scaffolding and others that lend themselves to more opportunities for enrichment. Each unit includes a focus term and additional vocabulary supports throughout the lessons. You can also find helpful links and suggestions for extending the learning at the end of each chapter. Throughout the teaching notes, invitations and permission to make this content your own and to expand and compress lessons based on the unique needs and context of your class communities.

Thank you for your interest in bringing more Women's and Gender Studies lessons to the middle school classroom. With you, we (Kathryn and Jill) share a belief that this work matters, that young people matter, and that together we can co-create a more just world.

The book you are holding is not a complete curriculum. On their own, these units do not correct for all the missing voices and histories; they do not solve global challenges. However, we hope they are seeds for this work. The book you are holding comes to life in what happens off the page, in the discussions, projects, and initiatives of you and your scholars. As the ancient Taoist proverb says, "A journey of a thousand miles begins with a single step." May these units be powerful first steps, conceptual catalysts, and inspirational sources that drive your classrooms forward to greater inclusion, action, and representation.

Why WGST?

Advisory Editor Concept Foreword by Dr. Elisa Glick

Dr. Elisa Glick *(she/her) is an associate professor of English and Women's and Gender Studies at the University of Missouri, where she teaches courses on feminist and queer theory, sexual and gender diversity, queer literature and culture, and 20th-century literary and artistic culture. She has published in the fields of gender and queer studies, most notably her book* Materializing Queer Desire: Oscar Wilde to Andy Warhol. *Elisa has expertise in feminist, anti-racist, and equity-focused pedagogies and is the founder of Mizzou's Faculty Institute for Inclusive Teaching. A diversity, equity, and inclusion consultant and the owner of Elisa Glick Consulting, she works with schools, colleges, and universities to help them build more inclusive and equitable classrooms and create sustainable change. Elisa holds a PhD in English from Brown University. She lives in Columbia, Missouri, with Carolyn Sullivan, her spouse and life partner of almost 30 years.*

I never set out to be a Women's and Gender Studies Professor or a feminist theorist. But looking back on my own academic journey, I think these are the spaces I most felt at home because I was able to bring all of who I am to my teaching and scholarship. For the first time, I felt welcomed into a supportive and mind-expanding community of learners, teachers, and activists who respected and cultivated difference, openness, nonconformity, ambiguity,

DOI: 10.4324/9781003289500-2

emotion, queerness, and pleasure. This is the kind of inspiring and transformative community that *Teaching Women's and Gender Studies: Classroom Resources on Resistance, Representation, and Radical Hope (Grades 6–8)* invites us into—a brave space of connection, trust, and justice grounded in the shared learning experience of WGST teachers and students.

Teaching Women's and Gender Studies breaks new ground by introducing the interdisciplinary field of WGST to the K-12 classroom, providing an accessible yet conceptually sophisticated roadmap that enables both educators and young people to become change agents for justice. In their first chapter "Why WGST?," Jill Clingan and Kathryn Fishman-Weaver not only deftly introduce the major concepts, issues, and problems in the field, but they also highlight their relevance to contemporary debates about social inequalities that disproportionately impact communities of color, Indigenous peoples, and LGBTQIA+ communities in national and transnational contexts. As a tenured professor who has taught and published in WGST and Queer Studies for the past 20 years, it's clear to me young people are leading the way to radically transform notions of gender and feminism. It's therefore especially fitting that, in the chapter that follows, Jill and Kathryn recognize and honor the individual and collective wisdom of young people while providing them with the necessary tools to increase their knowledge of WGST and what it has to offer increasingly diverse Gen Z learners.

"Why WGST?" offers a thematic focus that explores both differences and shared connections between and among feminist frameworks, distilling for readers some of the most complex and important insights in the field today. One of the key takeaways for students is there is far more diversity within feminism than is commonly recognized. Disrupting linear narratives of feminist "waves" that often privilege Western, White, middle class, cishet women, the chapter emphasizes that there is no single identity for or history of "feminist," "feminism," or "Women's and Gender Studies." Although they provide definitions of influential feminist movements and theories, the authors do not primarily aim to offer a survey of different feminist frameworks. Building on the assertion of multiple feminisms rather than a singular feminism, the chapter aims to (1) demonstrate the strengths of WGST as a mode of knowledge production grounded in lived experience; (2) introduce students to gender as a socially-constructed category of analysis and WGST as a discipline that uses a gender lens to deconstruct dominant paradigms; (3) examine how social inequalities and resistances shape forms of activism around the globe; (4) introduce students to contemporary feminism's most influential concept, intersectionality, a framework for understanding how multiple identities and systems of oppressions intersect; (5) increase awareness of and reflection on social location and the diverse impacts of power and privilege for individuals and communities; and (6) provide experiential learning activities so that practitioners can develop the critical consciousness necessary to become advocates and changemakers for justice. For me, the project of Women's and Gender Studies has always been the work of imagining and building a more inclusive, equitable, and just future. Both educators and students will find in "Why WGST?" not only new knowledge and skills but also—to quote the poet and feminist activist Adrienne Rich (2003)—"a new, expanded sense of what's humanly possible" (p. 26).

Teaching Concept Overview—Why WGST?

Purpose: These opening units introduce core WGST concepts and connect those to justice work locally and globally. In addition to broadly overviewing many feminisms and concepts, scholars also engage in research around the United Nations' fifth Sustainable Development Goal and map these targets to advocacy work in their local communities. Finally, scholars consider their own lived experiences, identities, and perceptions of feminisms and gender. This is deeply reflective work on which your class communities can continue to build throughout subsequent units.

✔ **Objectives**

By the end of these units, scholars will be able to:

◆ Connect the United Nations SDG 5 to local advocacy work.
◆ Define many types of feminisms and start to identify theories and methodologies they resonate with.
◆ Explain some of the nuances of gender as a social construct and name specific ways groups and individuals have expanded our understanding of gender.
◆ Analyze texts by feminist scholars, including bell hooks, Sojourner Truth, Emma Watson, and Chimamanda Adichie.
◆ Interview an elder on gender advocacy.

? Essential Questions for Scholars

◆ What can I learn about gender justice from transnational and global perspectives?
◆ How does the way gender is socially constructed affect my peers and me?
◆ What does feminism and justice mean to me?

⏸ Reflective Questions for Educators

◆ What justice issues (local and global) are centered in my curriculum?
◆ How can I advance greater gender, racial, ethnic, and linguistic representation in my curricular choices?
◆ How can my teaching contribute to further global awareness and student-led projects related to equity and justice?

Activate Prior Knowledge—Feminist T-Shirts	
Unit 1—Feminist Theory: Introduction	**Unit 2—We Can All Be Changemakers for Justice**
Lesson 1—United Nations' SDG 5: Exploration Lesson 2—What is WGST? Lesson 3—"Two Spirit": Gender as a Social Construct	Lesson 1—Ain't I A Woman?: Sojourner Truth Lesson 2—If Not You, Who? Sowing the Seeds of Advocacy Lesson 3—Feminisms Are for Everybody: bell hooks
Synthesis Project—WGST & Me	

Concept 1—Dedications

Kathryn's Dedication—I dedicate this section to a young person we'll call Mae.[1] A month or so into her ninth grade year, Mae asked me if she could talk to me about something. We found a quiet corner in the counselor's office. She said she had been reading about mental health in the LGBTQIA+ community. Over the next four years, she would continue to bring pertinent research to our classroom so that we could learn together. Mae said she knew it was important to identify safe and caring adults with whom she could be fully herself. She then told me that she is nonbinary and uses the pronouns "she/them."

What they said next is one of the most important things a student has ever said to me: "If I only talk to one person about my identity this year, I think it should be you."

With hope, Mae's words will always stick with me. I chose them for my chapter dedication because their message speaks to how much teachers matter. I also chose them because Mae actively asked for more Women's and Gender Studies coursework in their high school experience. They helped organize a research study on feminism at our high school and presented that work to graduate students at a university symposium. In short, Mae believed in this project before Jill and I had even dreamt it up.

While working with Jill on these lessons, I thought of Mae and several other bright young people who have participated in student-led advocacy projects with me over the years. I didn't think of Mae as she is now, a vibrant professional, confident, and successful in her various endeavors, but as she was in her teenage years, when she was seeking more representative lessons in her classes and more inclusive practices in our school. We (Kathryn and Jill) want to deliver on that wish and want to do so with tools, strategies, and vocabulary to support you in teaching toward a more inclusive world.

Jill's Dedication—I would like to dedicate this section to my daughter, Amélie. As I write this dedication, Amélie is a first-year student at the University of Missouri, Kansas City. Along with being a student, she is working, living on her own, and managing it all with a mix of tangled anxiety and beautiful confidence. Just as my heart feels a bit splintered since she has left home, it also brims with pride at who she has become and who she is becoming.

In this book, we (Jill and Kathryn) often reference those upon whose shoulders we stand in this important, expansive work of gender equity. Often, this refers to the shoulders of our ancestors, and while I, too, stand on the shoulders of those who have gone before me, I stand, at least as much, upon my daughter's shoulders. As I work with Kathryn on the lessons in this book, I so often think of Amélie and am inspired by her. She is an advocate for gender equity and intersectional justice and is a champion of inclusion. She is living a story of courage and compassion, and her story invites me to live my own story, as an educator and a human, with courage and compassion, as well.

When I think of the scholars that these two units will reach, I think of my daughter. I want to write lessons that she would have loved as a high school student. I want to write lessons that would have resonated with her own story. I want to write lessons that would have expanded the ideas of the other scholars in her school. I want to write lessons that could have bolstered her courage and confidence.

When I think of the scholars that these two units will reach, I also think of **you**. It was Amélie's middle school and high school teachers who truly helped her settle into who she is and who inspired within her the courage to live her own story. They loved her, encouraged her, gave her a safe space to retreat to, and filled their snack drawers with her favorite flavor of Pop-Tarts. We (Kathryn and I) hope to share tools and strategies with you as you help students live out their stories of courage and compassion, justice, and inclusion. This section introducing Women's and Gender Studies to your scholars will hopefully lay a foundation for those stories to be both told and lived.

Concept Introduction by Kathryn and Jill

You are a vibrant constellation of identities, experiences, and cultures. You may be living out the boldest dreams of your ancestors. And you are here, engaging in teaching and learning about Women's and Gender Studies. Like us (Kathryn and Jill), you likely believe that this work matters, that young people matter, that together we can co-create a more just world. Across the following units, you will remind scholars that they, too, are a vibrant constellation of identities, experiences, and cultures. They are the boldest dreams of their ancestors. They are here and can be leaders in co-creating a more just world.

We (Kathryn and Jill) believe that Women's and Gender Studies calls us to:

◆ think critically across disciplines and points of view;
◆ offer and celebrate more complete stories of history, culture, and identity;
◆ affirm a multiplicity of lived experiences and perspectives; and
◆ work to further the cause of justice and equity while also reducing oppression and marginalization.

This is a lofty work in what is already a high-stakes profession. As educators ourselves, we know that teaching is heart- and head-heavy work. It asks so much of both teacher and learner—terms that are often interchangeable. For this reason, please see our letters of care and support at the start of each new teaching concept. We hope these letters offer you some encouragement for the noble task of teaching for a more just world, tips for navigating the unit content, and an invitation to make choices for the best interest of you and your scholars' well-being.

The following two units introduce core concepts from this book, including justice, feminism, representation, gender, inclusion, identity, and equity. They ask scholars to begin to consider their own lived experiences, identities, and perceptions. This process might be uncomfortable for some scholars, as their concepts of gender and feminism may be challenged. Other scholars may find in these lessons an expression of beliefs they could not quite articulate before or an outlet for passions they did not know how to pursue. In these units, our hope is for scholars to have the space for growth, reflection, questioning, stretching, and transformation. In these stage-setting units, scholars are introduced to the tension between celebrating a multiplicity of stories and recognizing a specific pattern of gendered experiences and discrimination. Throughout the book, scholars (and educators) may want to return to these early reflections, questions, and impressions to track change and personal growth.

Educator Letter for Concept 1—*It Should Be You*

Dear Valued Educator,

These letters are our gift to you. They are a connecting space for us (Kathryn and Jill) to share some moments thinking together about the chapter content and what care might look like **for you** in teaching these big important ideas. We hope these letters (1) offer grounding information about why this work, *your work in the classroom*, matters and (2) give you specific ideas for care strategies as you embark on this important work.

Your Work Matters

If these lessons stir up something important in your scholars, as we (Kathryn and Jill) hope they do, you may be that one adult a young person identifies as their safe person. The Trevor Project's 2020 National Survey on LGBTQ Youth Mental Health (n.d.) reports that these relationships, classroom conversations, and culture of support can literally save lives. They also report that this is urgent work.

- Forty percent of LGBTQ respondents seriously considered attempting suicide in the past 12 months, with more than half of transgender and nonbinary youth having seriously considered suicide.
- Sixty-eight percent of LGBTQ youth reported symptoms of generalized anxiety disorder in the past two weeks, including more than three in four transgender and nonbinary youth.
- Forty-six percent of LGBTQ youth report they wanted psychological or emotional counseling from a mental health professional but were unable to receive it in the past 12 months.

These statistics from the Trevor Project are an updated version of the research Mae (pp. 13) brought me several years ago. Mae read a report like this, wasn't sure what to do with it, and then brought it to a trusted teacher.

We suspect that you, too, will have scholar conversations that begin, "Can I tell you something?" and end with equal parts weight and light in your heart. These conversations can happen with any of your scholars. Every scholar in your classroom is navigating unique and complicated experiences. Teaching WGST is deeply personal work, and as such, it often leads to scholars giving you their weights and hopes. Because of this, we want to encourage you right here at the onset of these units to set up a care plan—for yourself.

Care Strategies for Educators

- **Who are the colleague allies that you can go to for problem solving and support?** Identity those folks now, and if possible, include someone from your school's mental health team on your list. You may also want to identify a partner teacher that you can co-teach some of these lessons with.

◆ **What does self-care mean for you?** Does it look like a quiet walk in the morning, a yoga class on Thursdays, or cooking a favorite meal? Name several things that bring you joy and calm and put two on your calendar for this week and every week that follows.

◆ **Why are you teaching WGST?** Spend some time reflecting on this question early in your class studies. Your answer may surprise you, inspire you, and even guide your teaching.

Thank you for engaging in this noble work. If we only reach one educator with this book, we think it should be you.

With admiration,

Kathryn and Jill

Activate Prior Knowledge—Feminist T-Shirts

Teaching Notes

The activity we use to activate prior knowledge requires honesty, courage, and ample reflective space. In this activity, scholars respond to three statements, reflect individually, and then share their ideas in a whole-class dialogue. Scholars are asked to defend (agree), refute (disagree), or qualify (clarify or revise) each of the statements. Regardless of the position they choose, scholars are also asked to justify this position. This structure invites critical thinking and multiple answers and honors the wide range of perspectives in your class.

Before holding the dialogue, remind scholars of any class ground rules or norms you use in your work together, such as assuming positive intent, recognizing that all experiences are valid, practicing courage, and monitoring patterns of participation. Norms that reinforce that all voices and experiences have value in this conversation are essential to an inclusive politics in your classroom and feminist discourse around these ideas. Some of your scholars may have a background in feminisms and already be engaged in justice work. These experiences are important in this conversation. However, so, too, are the experiences of scholars who have not yet had access to feminism scholarship, had to think deeply about gender before, or who do not yet see themselves as leaders and changemakers (recognizing that there may be many reasons for this). As an educator, you can invite and affirm a multiplicity of voices in each of these lessons.

After scholars have had the opportunity to reflect individually, facilitate a classwide dialogue on these statements. Remind scholars there is no *right answer* to these questions. All of the perspectives and experiences that scholars bring to our class and to this activity can help deepen our collective learning. Invite scholars to share their justifications. On the surface, most people (though not all) agree with most of the content in the initial three statements. However, as we peel back the layers and share questions, quandaries, and corrections, this conversation becomes more critical and more complex. For example, statement 1, "Girls and women should have access to the same opportunities as boys and men," is an opportunity to ask how trans and nonbinary people are included (or excluded) in this statement.

Following this opener, scholars will then design their own feminist t-shirts. These shirts offer a creative way for scholars to share what feminism and justice mean to them. There should be as many different t-shirt designs as there are scholars in your class. How each student identifies and the experiences each student brings to your class matter. As scholars share their designs, remind them that in this space, we honor that all experiences are valid. As you dive into this content, create space to acknowledge assumptions, complicated feelings, questions, and biases you and your classes have around the term: *feminism*. You may personally find you have some of these beliefs and discomfort even if you fundamentally believe in affirming the rights and opportunities of all genders.

Over the next two units, your class will connect these statements to both the United Nations SDG 5 and feminist movements. This may lead to some big questions about gender, bias, equity, and justice.

As our class community begins to engage with these lessons on Women's and Gender Studies, take a moment to analyze the beliefs you hold about empowerment, opportunity, and equity. To start this conversation, read and consider each statement below. These statements are informed by the United Nations SDG 5.

Term	Definition
United Nations Sustainable Development Goals (SDGs)	The United Nations' Sustainable Development plan outlines 17 goals called the SDGs for peace, prosperity, and wellbeing for humanity and the planet we share. While gender threads across all SDGs, SDG 5 focuses directly on gender equality and empowerment.

Mark whether you would defend (agree), refute (disagree), or qualify (clarify or revise) these three statements. Then write your justifications (rationale) for your decisions. Some of these statements may bring up big feelings or questions for you. If so, note those and any reflections, as well.

	Statement	Defend, Refute, Qualify	Reflection and Justification
1	Girls and women should have access to the same opportunities as boys and men.		✎
2	It is important to work for the social, economic, and political equality of the sexes.		✎
3	All people (including children) should live in a world where they feel safe in their homes, neighborhoods, and communities.		✎

These three statements guide the work of the United Nations' Sustainable Development Goal 5, which is to *Achieve gender equality and empower all women and girls* (United Nations, n.d.-b). They also are core feminist beliefs.

Feminist T-Shirts

One of my (Kathryn's) alumna scholars, whom we'll call Jasmyn, was home from college during her winter break. She stopped by to see me, and we visited over coffee. I asked about her science classes, extracurriculars, and the latest books she was reading. She answered and then sharply turned our conversation to feminism. Jasmyn was frustrated with a lack of depth in the ways her peers talked about and practiced feminism.

> I mean, everyone gets a feminist t-shirt before the semester starts. Obviously, I can't imagine anyone at my school saying that they weren't a feminist, but you know most people aren't really *doing* anything about feminism. Like, if you're going to get a t-shirt that says you're a feminist, shouldn't you be working toward racial justice, inclusion for LGBTQIA+ students on campus, or volunteering at your local health clinic to help address health disparities?

Jasmyn was engaging in all of these actions and more; however, if I were to mention that, she would be quick to turn the focus away from herself.

"Look," I can almost hear her saying, "If you are doing the work, you don't need a shirt, and if you aren't doing the work, the shirt doesn't mean anything."

I wasn't familiar with the feminist t-shirt events that Jasmyn kept mentioning, so I asked her about this. She told me that a couple days before fall semester each year, there is a big event on her school quad. The event includes live music, signups for student activities, and feminist t-shirts. She told me:

> Everyone gets one. They come in a variety of sayings, you know, like, *as strong as the woman next to me; feminism is the radical notion that women are people;* and *this is what a feminist looks like.* They're all great messages. I just want it to mean something to the wearer.

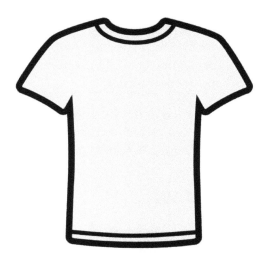

Jasmyn thought the t-shirts themselves were fine but only if they translated to action. This begs an interesting question to consider. *What would your feminist t-shirt say?* What is a value, commitment, or challenge you feel so strongly about that you would not only wear it on your person but also put it into action in the choices you make in your community? You do not have to choose one of the phrases listed above or any other phrase you have seen on a t-shirt. Be authentic to your core values. Take a moment to design your own feminist shirt and then share with a peer why you chose that message, quote, or phrase.

You might use these questions to process together:

◆ What did you think about while drawing?
◆ What does your feminist t-shirt say about what you believe and value?
◆ To borrow from Jasmyn's wisdom, how will you make this shirt *mean something*?
◆ If we could print these shirts tomorrow, would you wear them? Why or why not?

Closer. To close this activity, review the first three statements, reflect on our conversation in class today, and then respond to these last two statements using our same protocol from the start of class.

	Statement	Defend, Refute, Qualify	Reflection and Justification
4	The United Nations Sustainable Development Goal 5—*to achieve gender equality and empower all girls and women*—is an important and worthwhile goal.		✎
5	Feminism is for everybody.		✎

Unit 1—Feminist Theory: Introduction

As our early lessons and experiences in both the classroom and the world suggest, there is a lot of confusion about what feminism means, who feminism is for, and how these ideals might function in our communities and change movements. Throughout this book, we study feminist scholars and activists and their work around race, gender, identity, access, voice, and advocacy. These big concepts are often grounded in the everyday context of our lived experiences. In this text, we define feminism as *an affirmation of humanity that seeks freedom from oppression and commits to the full access of social, economic, and political rights and opportunities for all people*. Throughout these lessons, scholars will learn more about multiple feminist frameworks and feminisms, including radical feminisms, Black feminisms, queer theory, and transnational and global feminisms. As they do, scholars and educators will be able to build a feminist politic grounded in their own lived experiences, unique views, and commitments.

In this opening unit, scholars consider the multiplicity of identities, stories, and experiences that contribute to specific patterns related to discrimination, access, representation, and safety. This unit introduces core concepts including justice, feminism, gender, inclusion, and equity. As we consider the global scale of feminist work, scholars explore the United Nations SDG 5 on gender equality and empowerment seeking to better understand how human rights and opportunities are affirmed or denied. In addition to looking out at global issues, scholars also look in to examine their own lived experiences, identities, and perceptions of feminism and gender.

We (Kathryn and Jill) don't expect or require that all scholars identify as feminists. We do, however, aim to create contexts where scholars are inspired to work toward equity and justice, where they bring forward critical challenges related to inclusion and representation, and where they feel empowered to lead actions focused on ending injustice and oppression.

Key Term: *Lived Experiences*

Have you heard the phrase *no one does you better than you*? An extension of this phrase may be *no one knows you and your experiences better than you*. Lived experiences are the primary source account of the experiences, choices, everyday activities, and knowledge a person has gained through their direct involvement with the world.

Focusing on lived experiences emphasizes that you are the most qualified person to report on your lives and experiences. Further, your experiences are a source of knowledge. In 1970, Carol Hanisch published an article titled, "The personal is political." This deep-seated belief that

---

our lived experiences hold knowledge and map against collective trends, including structural oppression and challenges, is a cornerstone of many of the feminist theories we study in the following lessons.

These lessons emphasize that all experiences are valid, that people are experts on their own lives, and that personal stories have the power to build bridges and increase understanding.

Related Term: *Intersectionality*

Intersectionality is a framework for understanding how multiple identities and *systems of oppressions* intersect to create specific experiences and conditions within systems. These experiences include systems of advantage (power and privilege) and disadvantage (discrimination and oppression). For example, these may include the compounding effects of racism and sexism or racism and heterosexism or racism, sexism, and heterosexism. This framework centers the experiences and "voices of those experiencing overlapping, concurrent forms of oppression in order to understand the depths of the inequalities and the relationships among them in any given context" (UN Women, 2020, para 5). Recognizing the first-person experiences and stories of individuals from historically marginalized and multiply marginalized backgrounds as important sites for knowledge is inherent to intersectional approaches. (See also descriptions of *Black feminisms* that we explore throughout this book.)

Related Term: *Asset-Based Approaches*

Asset-based approaches, also called *strengths-based approaches*, seek to recognize and leverage the unique skills, talents, and strengths of individuals and communities. These approaches acknowledge that while systems or institutions may be broken or in need of repair, people bring genius, talents, and inherent worth to our communities.

Teaching Notes

Mature Content—Sexual Violence

Over the next two lessons, scholars will explore the United Nations SDG 5 targets, which include some difficult content around violence and sexual violence. We (Kathryn and Jill) know that different school communities and grade bands will have different guidelines about addressing this content in class. We also know that this topic may be personally triggering to individual scholars and educators.

To keep this lesson as accessible as possible, we did not include some of the more difficult language around female genital mutilation in our lesson materials; however, scholars may find this in their own research. With middle school scholars, you may want to point them to specific, vetted resources that are appropriate for your class community. Likewise, in the Adichie speech, "We Should All be Feminists," there is a reference to a gang rape. The reference is brief and you could fast forward through it without missing the speaker's overall meaning.

As always, you are best able to make decisions about what content is appropriate for the scholars in your classes.

For those who do choose to teach about how sexual violence, violence against women, and female genital mutilation fit within the United Nations' Sustainable Development Goals, we encourage you to proceed with caution and humanity. Below are four important reminders for this work.

◆ Avoid any victim-blaming language. The perpetrators of violence against women are to blame for violence against women. Full stop.

◆ Guard against ethnocentrism or us/them language. Gender-based violence is not something that happens "in other places." It is a danger we all live with in every community.

◆ Scholars may have anatomical questions related to this content. I (Kathryn) find it helpful to lean on my peers in health and science education for these conversations. When I taught in public high schools, I frequently invited supportive biology and anatomy teachers to my classroom to field scholars' questions and help me facilitate the scientific parts of these conversations.

◆ Finally, remember that educators do not know all of the lived experiences of their scholars. Be upfront about the topics you will cover before diving into the content. Give scholars permission to take care of themselves, to take a break, and to go speak with a counselor. Remind scholars that you also are a safe person to process with if they need to share something difficult that this lesson may have brought up. Also give yourself permission to take care of yourself, including seeking support for any feelings this content may stir up in you.

Mandated Reporting—Many of you are also *mandated reporters*. This means when and if young people bring you experiences of abuse, neglect, or immediate danger, there is a system of reporting that you are legally required to put in place. To support you in the moment of these difficult situations, here is a modified script I (Kathryn) have used in my work with young people in these cases:

Oh, [NAME], that took so much courage to share. Thank you for trusting me with this difficult story. I also need you to know that because this experience is affecting your safety, we will have to bring another person into this conversation. I will be right here with you the whole time. Do you have an administrator or counselor that you trust? If so, let me know, and I'll arrange that conversation. In the meantime, you can stay right here with me. [NAME], I care about you and want to keep you safe.

While the young person can't decide whether or not you report the information, you can still look for opportunities for agency and commit to care and transparency throughout the process.

Navigating the responsibility and weight of hotlining an abuse incident is challenging for educators, too. It is also not something you have to do on your own. You can report with a counselor or administrator. Many districts have an "employee assistance program" that covers confidential therapy support for educators. A mentor of mine recently shared that he recommends scheduling a therapy conversation for yourself anytime you have to report abuse. I (Kathryn) think this is brilliant advice. By taking care of your own mental health, you are more able to take care of the mental health of your students.

Lesson 1: United Nations' SDG 5—Exploration

 Thought Questions

- What makes an issue a local issue?
- What makes an issue a global issue?
- For example, is food insecurity a local issue or a global issue?
- What about gender-based discrimination?

These issues, like all issues we will explore in these lessons, are complex. They are both global and local. Engaging in justice work requires us to look deeply at both how issues map across contexts and what this means in local contexts, including our own schools and communities.

In this opening lesson, you will explore gender-related issues that the United Nations has named important for our global community. Before diving into these issues, we want to introduce the terms *global feminisms* and *transnational feminisms*.

Term	Definition
Global feminisms	The intentional study of feminisms from around the world. This study is grounded in an ethics of inclusion. Global feminisms explore local feminisms and justice movements, transnational approaches (or those that move beyond geographical boundaries), and global trends such as those in the United Nations SDGs. The Vanderbilt Global Feminisms Collaborative (n.d.) writes: Global feminisms scholars are engaged in the study of boundaries associated with sex, gender, sexuality, class, race, ability, ethnicity, geography, identity, and membership—using both theoretical and empirical lenses. They are attentive to silence and marginalization, to citizenship politics (including migration, refugees, rights, and participation), to political economy (formal and informal), to society and culture, and to the environment (understood as the places where we live, work, play, and pray). (para 3)

Term	Definition
Transnational feminisms	A methodology that seeks global action and understanding. It strives to move beyond individual nations or nation-states to engage in a more collective production of knowledge.

As you explore feminist frameworks throughout the following lessons, think critically about the claims being made and the context in which they are made. See if you can identify inherent blind spots or biases in how information is presented. Everyone has blind spots and biases. One of the objectives of these WGST lessons is to help you see these more clearly so that you can fill gaps in understanding and work to reduce your own biases. Critiques matter—they push each of us toward that next best version. And yet, you can also spend too much time in criticism. After a certain period of wrestling with a new idea, a grounding question to come back to is this: *How can I use this idea to further the cause of justice?*

"Rather than asking what transnational feminism *is*," Asha Nadkarni and Subhalakshmi Gooptu (2017) write, "it is more useful to think about what transnational feminist theorizing *does* or makes possible" (para 1). As you explore the United Nations' Sustainable Development Goals, focus on solutions, actions, and advocacy. Recognizing that these issues are both local and global, pay attention to context, nuance, and the different realities of the various communities you are exploring, including your own local and school communities.

Name _____   Date _____

Directions: Working in teams, select one of the focus priorities below and create a six-slide presentation for your peers. Your slides should address the following:

◆ What area of gender justice is your team focused on?
◆ What United Nations targets does this relate to? Define all key terms that might be unfamiliar to your peers.
◆ Name one important global trend related to this issue.
◆ Identify a local (school or city) connection to this issue and an organization or person who is working for positive change.
◆ How could you and your peers support this work?
◆ Cite your sources.

Later, you will have the opportunity to learn with classmates who researched a different priority. You can use the chart below to take notes during your peers' presentations.

Used with permission from Fishman-Weaver and Clingan, Teaching Women's and Gender Studies. Copyright © 2023, Taylor and Francis, Inc.

Exploring United Nations' Sustainable Development Goal 5

Achieve gender equality and empower all women and girls.

Key Point	Topics	United Nations Targets	Notes
Expand equality and end discrimination.	Nondiscrimination, voting, legislation, and empowerment	End discrimination against women and girls (5.1). Adopt and strengthen policies and enforceable legislation for gender equality (5.C).	
Expand reproductive health and end violence.	Physical and psychological safety, reproductive health care, education	End all violence and exploitation against women and girls (5.2). Eliminate forced and child marriages (5.3). Universal access to reproductive rights and health (5.6).	
Create equal leadership and economic opportunities.	Politics, decision making, leadership, property	Ensure full participation in leadership and decision-making (5.5). Equal rights to economic resources, property ownership and financial services (5.A).	
Expand mobility and value domestic work.	Mobile telephone ownership, household, family	Promote empowerment of women through technology (5.B). Value unpaid care and promote shared domestic responsibilities (5.4).	

Sources: United Nations, SDG Tracker; United Nations SDG 5

Used with permission from Fishman-Weaver and Clingan, Teaching Women's and Gender Studies. Copyright © 2023, Taylor and Francis, Inc.

Teaching Notes

This lesson introduces scholars to a definition of both Women's and Gender Studies and feminism. In this text, we (Jill and Kathryn) define *feminism* as *an affirmation of humanity that seeks freedom from oppression and commits to the full access of social, economic, and political rights and opportunities for all people*. This is a layered definition! Scholars have already begun thinking about what feminism is by exploring SDG 5 and creating their own feminist t-shirts. Now, they will work collaboratively to break down this definition of feminism into its component parts and analyze what each part means to them and to their peers. As with the SDG activity, remind scholars that there is not a singular "right way" to fill in this chart. In fact, the multiplicity of perspectives and experiences that each scholar brings to the dialogue creates a rich space for exploration, thought, and discussion.

You could create a large anchor chart with this definition and have scholars populate the chart with Post-it notes. This can also work online, as well. When we (Kathryn and Jill) facilitated this activity with a group of educators, we shared a Google Doc of this chart, and educators spent a few moments populating the chart with their ideas about how to unpack each component of the definition. Then we talked through this brainstorm together.

This chart can serve as an important and living reference as you and your scholars explore these lessons. Having it accessible throughout the units may serve as a helpful teaching tool.

Lesson 2: What Is WGST?

Name _____ Date_____

> **Women's and Gender Studies (WGST)**—An interdisciplinary study of the ways gender is constructed and how it affects our lived experiences and opportunities; a commitment to work toward greater justice and equity; and the intentional centering of stories, histories, and contributions of women and girls that are too often missing from curricula and media.

 Thought Question

◆ In reading this definition of Women's and Gender Studies, what surprises or interests you?

Women's and Gender Studies (WGST) spans the arts, humanities, social sciences, and sciences. Throughout the lessons in this book, we focus on three main aspects of Women's and Gender Studies.

◆ **Analysis**—How is gender constructed, and in what ways do those beliefs affect our lived experiences and opportunities?
◆ **Advocacy**—How can we work toward greater justice, equality, and equity?
◆ **Representation**—In what areas do we need to work toward greater gender representation? How can we center and celebrate more contributions, stories, and histories?

Activating Prior Knowledge—Women's and Gender Studies

You and your peers bring important knowledge, experiences, and background to these themes. On the following page is a chart to fill out in small groups.

Start Where You Are—Feminism

Name_____ Date_____

Scholar Chart—Let's break down this definition into its components. What does each part mean to you and your peers?[2]

Feminism: An affirmation of humanity that seeks freedom from oppression and commits to the full access of social, health, economic, and political rights and opportunities for all people.

Affirmation of humanity	Freedom from oppression	Social rights and opportunities	Health rights and opportunities	Economic rights and opportunities	Political rights and opportunities	For all people

Used with permission from Fishman-Weaver and Clingan, Teaching Women's and Gender Studies. Copyright © 2023, Taylor and Francis, Inc.

Equity and *equality* are two terms you will come across throughout this book, and while they may sound similar, they are actually quite different. While some feminist movements, including liberal feminisms, have fought for equality of rights and opportunities, others, such as radical feminisms and Black feminisms, have fought for equity.

Equality means everyone receives the same regardless of need. For example, let's imagine that a school principal recently learned that two of her eighth graders were having a hard time reading the fine print in their English literature text. In response, she wrote a grant for free reading glasses for all eighth graders at her school. This kind of equality approach sounds great—free reading glasses for everyone, and it might help the two students who were having a hard time with the text, as well as others who are slightly nearsighted. However, the reading glasses would offer insufficient correction for people who are farsighted or visually impaired, and they would be a nuisance to people with very strong vision. Further, if young people have other obstacles to literacy education, including learning disabilities, the reading glasses wouldn't help and would even be a waste of resources. This isn't to say that all approaches grounded in equality are problematic; some have been very important. For example, in my (Kathryn's) local school district, administrators now give *all* scholars and families information about accessing free and reduced-price lunches. This is a change from when families used to have to opt in to receive the information or counselors had to reach out to specific individuals they thought might benefit from the information. By making the same information available to all, the school district is able to better support families who may be moving in and out of food insecurity.

Equity, on the other hand, looks deeply at systems to determine needs and root causes of injustice to consider how local and individual context affects challenges and solutions. An equity approach to this same challenge with the two eighth graders might be to survey the grade 8 class to learn who else is struggling with the text and who is excelling. It might involve getting reading glasses or a large print version for the initial two scholars, but it may also reveal that there is a small group of recent immigrants who need more language intervention. Rather than using resources to give everyone the same resource (e.g. reading glasses), this approach seeks to look deeply at systems, identify specific needs, and respond to those contextualized needs so that everyone has an opportunity to thrive. In the free-and-reduced-lunch example, an equity approach might go even further to consider additional wrap-around services such as access to food banks, pantries, and weekend snack packs, as well as health and economic supports related to hunger.

During your studies, you will encounter many new vocabulary terms like these. Below are five key concepts we have started exploring in these early WGST lessons.

Term	Definition
Equality	Having the same status, rights, and opportunities.
Equity	Fairness and justice; equity is different from equality (see above) in that it recognizes that different people have different experiences, opportunities, access, and needs—because of this, equity work requires systematic change to remove barriers, adjust imbalances, and create more just solutions and systems
Feminism	Freedom from oppression, an affirmation of humanity, and a commitment to the full access of social, economic, health, and political rights and opportunities for all people (See also the definitions and discussion of Black feminisms, transnational and global feminisms, queer theory, liberal feminisms, and radical feminisms.)
Gender	Socially constructed and culturally specific roles, behaviors, and identities of being feminine, masculine, or a combination of traits
Sex	A label (female or male) assigned at birth based on reproductive anatomy, chromosomes, and biology.
Scholarship	The academic study of and/or commitment to learning at a high level.

Vocabulary Connections

Reflect on your SDG 5 research presentations. Connect some of these vocabulary words to your research on that activity.

Term	Reflection Question
Equality	How does *equality* affect the issues or solutions you explored?
Equity	How does *equity* affect the issues or solutions you explored?
Equality vs. equity	Do you believe it is more important to work for equality or equity on this issue? Defend your answer with specific examples.
Feminism and justice	How is justice, including social or racial justice, embedded in the issue you studied?
Scholarship	How is *scholarship* important in advancing work on this issue? Offer specific examples.

Lesson 3: "Two Spirit"—Gender as a Social Construct

Teaching Note

This unit introduces the idea that gender is a social construct. This concept is typically new for middle school scholars and can lead to important conversations about the differences between sex (biology) and gender (culture). The lesson is divided into four distinct parts. Depending on the conversation following each section, you may find you need an extra class period or two to work through this content together.

◆ First, scholars are briefly introduced to ideas about the ways gender is socially constructed. This introduction invites scholars to imagine new possibilities and to celebrate a multiplicity of identities.

◆ Next is a short dialogue that builds on gender as a social construct. This dialogue is written in a more casual tone to invite scholars to ask similar candid questions as they explore these new concepts.

◆ Third, scholars review lesson vocabulary related to gender-expansive identities. If you have a GSA (gay-straight alliance) or other similar student group, you might invite the faculty sponsor to help you facilitate questions and clarifications about these terms.

◆ The lesson ends with readings on gender identities beyond the binary including two-spirit traditions in Native American Indigenous communities, *the kathoey* in Thailand, and *the hijra* in India. Depending on your class, you may want to read these aloud to everyone so that you can respond together and so that you are available to help with questions. We have also provided a PCR (prior knowledge-connections-research) chart to accompany this lesson and help scholars organize their notes. Throughout these readings, scholars consider how colonization has oppressed and restricted gender expression and more expansive identities. This last section offers the possibility for strong social studies connections on the harm and destruction caused by colonization, violence, and settler politics across Indigenous communities worldwide.

Simone de Beauvoir famously said, "One is not born, but rather becomes a woman." In this quote, de Beauvoir is referring to the difference between sex and gender, namely that gender is constantly being negotiated and constructed. Judith Butler (1956–), an American philosopher and gender theorist, whose book *Gender Trouble* (1990 followed by a second edition in 1999) remains a seminal queer theory text, writes that these categories and identities related to gender have the potential to be unmade and remade; however, because they are rooted in systems of power, acts of resistance carry risk.

These lessons invite you to imagine and celebrate new possibilities. In Concept 2, you will explore how joy can be a form of resistance. Pride, also, can be an act of resistance. In this lesson, you will read about the bright expansiveness of gender and gender identity. This bright expansiveness holds true across time, geography, and culture. Gender and the ways an individual expresses their gender identity may be in concert or conflict with the cultural norms of specific communities and historical periods. These tensions between expectations, social constructs, and the vast range of experiences may reinforce ideas about gender, reject ideas about gender, or introduce new ideas about what it means to be human.

Gender Is a Social Construct—A Dialogue

Scholar 1: Today we learned about the ways gender is socially constructed.

Scholar 2: *What does that even mean? Are you saying that gender isn't real because gender feels pretty real to me?*

Scholar 2: Sure. Our social constructs give us real information. They guide our behavior, inform identity, and are often reinforced in dangerous ways. When social theorists say that gender is a social construct, they aren't saying that it isn't real. They are simply saying it isn't biologically determined or static. What gender means changes across time, culture, situation, and person.

Scholar 2: *Woah. Ummm. Not biologically determined? There are some biological differences between guys and gals.*

Scholar 1: Sure, there are some biological differences between the sexes (female, male, intersex, etc). However, sex and gender aren't the same thing.

Scholar 2: *Intersex?*

Scholar 1: Yep, lots of people are born with a reproductive anatomy that doesn't fit our limited binary definitions of female or male.

Scholar 2: *Lots of people?*

Scholar 1: We read a 2021 article by Amnesty International, which reported that about 1.7% of babies born are intersex. This is about the same number of babies born with red hair.

Scholar 2: *Well, if it's so common, why didn't I know about it before?*

Scholar 1: Once a social construct is created, it has to be socially reinforced to gain meaning. If, for example, part of our social construct for gender in the United States is that there are only two options, then individuals with genders, identities, or anatomical parts outside of this binary are often forced to the margins. Social constructs lose their power through non-examples.

> **Scholar 1**: *Oh. I see it. The same is probably true for my trans friends, huh?*
> **Scholar 2**: For sure. However, these constructs don't only limit the LGBTQIA+ community. They limit all of us. This is how we get a culture that teaches boys not to cry even when they are sad and girls not to be too loud even when they feel something strongly.
> **Scholar**: Yeah. . . .

Term	Definition
Social construct	An idea that has been created, accepted, and reinforced across a cultural group (e.g. gender and race).
Cisgender	People whose gender aligns with the sex they were assigned at birth. For example, if a baby was assigned male at birth and identifies as a boy/man, he would be considered cisgender (or cis).
Transgender	People whose gender does not align with the sex they were assigned at birth. For example, if a baby was assigned male at birth and later identifies as a girl/woman, she may be transgender (or trans).
Intersex	A general term used for a variety of situations in which a person's reproductive anatomy doesn't fit the binary definitions of "female" or "male."
Gender-expansive	An umbrella term for people whose gender expression and identity are beyond or outside a specific gender identity, category, or label. As an umbrella term, *gender-expansive* encompasses many different identities. Some gender-expansive people use this term when referencing their gender identity, and some prefer other related terms. For example, <ul><li>Some gender-expansive people identify with a spectrum of genders and may use the term *nonbinary*.</li><li>Some gender-expansive people identify primarily with a single gender and may use the term *transgender*,</li><li>and still other gender-expansive people may identify without a gender and use the term *agender*.</li><li>As with all identity labels, it is important to honor the terms and language individual's identify with while also respecting that language can change over time.</li></ul>

Because gender is a social construct, it is also culturally specific. The roles, behaviors, and identities considered appropriate for specific genders vary across cultures and over time. As we continue in our learning, we will explore some of these cultural differences in our study of *the kathoey* from Thailand, "two-spirit" people in the Navajo nations; *the hijra* in India; and trans, non-binary, gender nonconforming, and gender-expansive identities in our own communities and beyond.

Beyond the Binary: Lesson Notes (PCR)

Names _____ Date _____

	PRIOR KNOWLEDGE *What You Already Know*	CURIOSITIES *What You Want to Know*	RESEARCH *Questions and Sources to Explore*
Colonization			
Gender-expansive identities			
Thailand India Native cultures in the United States			

Used with permission from Fishman-Weaver and Clingan, Teaching Women's and Gender Studies. Copyright © 2023, Taylor and Francis, Inc.

Term	Definition
Colonization	To violently establish control over the Indigenous people of an area. This control is intended to benefit those coming to the land and colonizing, even at the great harm of those who have previously cared for and called the land home. In addition to physical harm, Indigenous traditions and culture are often devalued or destroyed during colonization.
Binary	Consisting of only two parts.

Many cultures have long recognized, revered, and celebrated more than two genders. In the next section, you will learn about gender identities that transcend binary definitions. These are just a few examples among many. Before beginning these readings, it is important to emphasize that gender and identity are vast. Further, this vastness is even more complex when considered across our global community (Pattanaik, 2019). The following short readings are *brief summaries*, meaning they offer a starting place and are also incomplete. Further, because these stories transcend culture and language, some of the terms and interpretations have been translated from their original context several times.[3] As you explore these examples, read with an open mind and heart, recognizing that your own experiences, culture, and language influence your worldview and your approach to new information.

Two-Spirit Identities—First Nations, North America

As least 150 pre-colonial Native American tribes acknowledged third genders in their communities (HRC Staff, 2020), and many Native American nations recognized five distinct genders. The roots of a limited and more restrictive gender binary can often be traced to colonization.

"Two spirit" is an umbrella term, originally introduced in 1990 in Winnipeg, Canada, as a means of unifying various gender identities and expressions (Enos, 2018). However, individual nations and tribes have distinct names for gender-expansive people, for example, the *winkte* among the Lakota and the *nadleeh* among the Navajo people (Enos, 2018). Two spiritpeople could often move freely between men and women, and many held important leadership and spiritual roles in their nations.

Colonization and other acts of violence against Native peoples resulted in the tragic loss of many Native traditions including two-spirit identities. However, there is a growing revitalization and resistance movement among two-spirit people and other LGBTQ+ Native people throughout North America to revive two-spirit roles and traditions (Indian Health Service, n.d.).

The Kathoey in Thailand

Legend suggests that the Thai system was always based on a model of the three genders: male, female, and kathoey (Holcomb, 2021). Kathoey are identified as male at birth and then transition to a feminine identity. This transition often occurs before puberty and is permanent. The kathoey are recognized as a socially acceptable identity.

Thailand is credited as being the most LGBTQ+ friendly country in East Asia (Mancino, 2019). There are three primary reasons for this. First is the presence of the kathoey: one in 166 men identify as kathoey (Mancino, 2019). The second reason is based on Thailand's history. Thailand is the only nation in the region to resist European colonization. Because of this resistance, they were able to hold onto their own cultural values and were less influenced by Eurocentric powers, including normative heterosexuality and binary gender. Third, Thailand is a Buddhist country, and a major tenant of Buddhism is acceptance.

Many kathoey work in entertainment, singing, performing, and acting. While the kathoey often experience marginalization professionally, there is a wider spread social acceptance of the kathoey than what is seen in the West. Several kathoeys hold prominent professional positions including Dr. Seri Wongmontha, Tanwarin Sukkhapisit, and Prempreeda Pramoj Na Ayutthaya who, in addition to their activism, serve in academics, politics, and for the United Nations Educational, Scientific, and Cultural Organization program, respectively. Several kathoey have also achieved national fame, including Treechada Petcharat, an actress and model who won several beauty pageants in 2004, and Parinya Charoenphol, a famous boxer.

Hijra in India

Drawing on verse from *The Ramayana*, which dates back to fourth century B.C., the Hindu legend says that when Lord Rama was exiled from Ayodhya, he told his disciples: "Men and women, please wipe your tears and go away." And so most left. However, a group of people who were neither men nor women stayed behind, at the edge of the forest (Gettleman, 2018). They were hijras, a specific gender identity. Many believe they have the power to bless or curse, which leads to social interactions mixed with both fear and entertainment. Although they are nationally recognized, hijra also have very few employment options. They are often forced to beg, crash ceremonies, or engage in sex work.

Hundreds of years ago, hijra were respected as a unique and valued group. However, when the British colonized India in the mid-1800s, they brought with them a strict and limiting belief system about sex, gender, and identity. Many scholars point to this as the start of homophobia and trans-discrimination in India (Gettleman, 2018). The hijra, who are not the only trans community in India, have specific cultural and community practices, including their own language, Hijra Farsi, which is a combination of Persian and Hindustani (Johari, 2014).

There have been some improvements for hijra in recent years. For example, confirmation surgeries can now be performed at some government hospitals. Further, transgender people are now recognized as an official third gender and are therefore eligible for social benefits, including welfare. There is a wide vocabulary for gender identities (see *Kinnar*, *Aravani*, and *Thirunangi*), and this nuance matters, as we know that much of the nuance is lost in attempting to translate this vocabulary for gender identities to English words or Western understandings. Finally, it is important to note that not all transgender people in India are also hijra.

Closing Thoughts

In this lesson, you explored the expansive nature of gender and gender identity. This expansiveness spans across time, geography, and culture. The vast range of experiences may have reinforced what you knew about gender, rejected what you knew about gender, and even introduced new ideas about what it means to be human. Take a reflective beat to respond to the following in your journal:

- ◆ What challenged you in this lesson?
- ◆ What inspired you in this lesson?
- ◆ What are you taking away from this lesson?

Unit 2—We Can All be Changemakers for Justice

What do you think of when you read the word *justice*? Your prior knowledge and lived experiences with equity, law, social justice, and the justice system may all affect your answer to this question. These complicated and varied answers matter. They also shed important light into the gaping distance between justice as a philosophy of love (see below) and practices that in the name of justice cause further harm and inequities. The United Nations Department of Economic and Social Affairs (2017) defines social justice as "the peaceful and prosperous coexistence within and among nations." What would it mean to have a peaceful and prosperous coexistence within and among all genders, peoples, and communities? Asked differently, what would it look like to live in a just world? As a scholarly community, these lessons ask you to wrestle deeply with this question and then strive wholeheartedly to make that vision a reality.

> **Key Term: *Justice***
>
> Feminist scholar and social justice advocate bell hooks (CNN—bell hooks, 2000) once said, "The greatest movement for social justice our country has ever known is the civil rights movement and it was totally rooted in a love ethic."
>
> Justice in its deepest sense is rooted in radical, inclusive love. In its purest form, it is fairness, equity, and humanity.
>
> ◆ How can fairness, equity, and a "love ethic" affirm humanity and free people from oppression (see the Start Where You Are activity on p. 32)?
>
> Tragically, many unjust things have been done in the name of justice. For this reason, it is essential to think critically about both philosophy and practice. In exploring justice work, you can use these questions as a starting place for analysis:
>
> ◆ What does justice mean in this context? Who is defining it?
> ◆ Is this practice furthering ethics and equity? If not, is it really justice?
>
> In the following lessons, we encourage you to unpack these layers, asking critical questions about how we can each teach and learn toward a more just world.

Related Term: *Racial Justice*

Racial justice seeks to repair the intergenerational trauma inflicted on communities of color. This work includes dismantling systemic racism and the structures that perpetuate racism and ongoing harm toward communities of color. Racial justice is grounded in action, advocacy, and antiracist education, which moves purposefully toward new sustainable systems and practices rooted in racial equity.

Lesson 1: "Ain't I A Woman?"—Sojourner Truth

More than 100 years after her passing, Sojourner Truth's legacy continues to influence justice work. She is revered as an influential feminist and abolitionist. Her work influenced Black feminisms (see Lesson 3 in this unit) and intersectionality (see the proseminar on pp. 165-175). In the following reading, you will learn more about Truth's life, her advocacy, and a few allies who supported her along the way. You will then analyze Truth's most famous speech, "Ain't I a Woman?" (1851).

Term	Definition
Advocacy	The act of supporting and working toward a specific cause, which can include organizing, educating, lobbying, training, and mobilizing.
Allyship	The active and intentional practice of being for a person or group of people to which you do not belong. Generally, allyship is when a person with more privilege or power in a specific area acts for or on behalf of those who are systematically marginalized or disempowered in that area. Allies continue to take action even when they are unsure of the outcome and/or when acting on behalf of this group carries personal risk. Allyship is about justice (We continue this discussion as an extension activity in Concept 3.)

Sojourner Truth (1797–1883)

Isabella Bomfree, who later changed her name to Sojourner Truth, was born into slavery at the end of the 18th century. Subjected to violence, abuse, and the dehumanizing practices of slavery, Truth was bought and sold several times throughout her childhood and young adult life. Additionally, she faced the trauma and cruelty of watching both her parents and children sold away from her.

Allyship—Shelter, Financial, and Legal Resources

The year before New York legislation ended slavery, Truth escaped with her youngest daughter to the shelter of Maria and Isaac Van Wagener, an abolitionist couple. The Van Wageners took Truth in and purchased freedom for her and her youngest daughter. They also helped her successfully sue for the return of her young son Peter who had been illegally sold into slavery (Michels, 2015). This was one of Truth's first experiences with legislative advocacy, a strategy she used in her work for racial and gender justice throughout her life. As an advocate, she went by the name Sojourner Truth, but she changed her legal name to Isabella Van Wagener (National Abolition Hall of Fame and Museum, n.d.).

Legal Action and Advocacy Work

◆ During the Civil War, Truth organized supplies for Black troops and supported the Union cause.

◆ Following the war, she was honored with an invitation from President Abraham Lincoln to come to the White House.

◆ In Washington, D.C., she worked with the Freedmen's Bureau to support formerly enslaved people find jobs.

◆ She lobbied against segregation including winning a case against a streetcar conductor who had violently blocked her from riding.

◆ Truth also collected thousands of signatures on a petition to provide formerly enslaved people with land; however, Congress never took action on this petition.

Allyship—Amplifying Voices

In 1850, Sojourner Truth dictated her memoir *The Narrative of Sojourner Truth* to Olive Gilbert. In addition to writing the memoir, Gilbert also assisted Truth with the publication of the book. Truth was able to live off her book royalties (Michels, 2015).

Although Truth never had access to the educational opportunities to learn to read or write, she navigated the legal system, advocated passionately, and lectured widely on abolitionist and women's rights causes, championing suffrage and racial justice. She also spoke both Dutch, her native language, and English.

Sojourner Truth believed that racial justice and women's rights were inexorably linked. Truth taught that racial justice would never be fully achieved until people fought as tirelessly for women's rights as they did for other justice causes. She frequently reminded audiences and advocates that Black women were half of the formerly enslaved and enslaved populations. She also stressed that abolition alone was not equivalent with freedom and liberation—the fight for justice must continue with a focus on resisting racism, promoting literacy, overcoming sexism, and eradicating all forms of prejudice. This work and Truth's legacy continue today.

Dialogue and Connect

◆ What examples of advocacy work can you identify in this reading? As you think about your own advocacy, what can you learn from Sojourner Truth?

◆ Review the definition of allyship. Why do you think the authors note that *allyship is about justice and not personal gain,* and how does that relate to this narrative?

"Ain't I A Woman?"

Sojourner Truth delivered her most famous speech, "Ain't I A Woman?" in 1851. Below is an excerpt from the most cited version of her speech which appeared in her autobiography. Read the excerpt and respond to the questions that follow.

That man over there says that women need to be helped into carriages, and lifted over ditches, and to have the best place everywhere. Nobody ever helps me into carriages, or over mud-puddles, or gives me any best place! And ain't I a woman?

Look at me! Look at my arm! I have ploughed and planted, and gathered into barns, and no man could head me! And ain't I a woman?

I could work as much and eat as much as a man—when I could get it—and bear the lash as well! And ain't I a woman?

I have borne thirteen children, and seen most all sold off to slavery, and when I cried out with my mother's grief, none but Jesus heard me! And ain't I a woman?

Think, Pair, Share

◆ Summarize Sojourner's Truth message in your own words. Why is this message important for both racial and gender justice?

◆ In 2014, bell hooks (see Lesson 3) published a book after Sojourner Truth's famous speech. Her book, titled *Ain't I a Woman: Black Women and Feminism,* centers the experiences of Black women and explores the intersection of racism, sexism, and discrimination as they have impacted Black women throughout U.S. history. Why do you think bell hooks chose to reference Sojourner Truth's speech in her title? In what ways does Truth's message continue to have relevance today?

Lesson 2: If Not You, Who? Sowing the Seeds of Advocacy

 Thought Question
- ◆ Who can work for the causes of gender justice and equity?
- ◆ How do gender stereotypes affect you and your peers?

In this lesson, scholars will analyze two speeches both calling for greater participation in feminist movements: "We Should All Be Feminists" by Chimamanda Adichie and "HeforShe" by Emma Watson. After listening to both speeches, encourage scholars to react, compare, contrast, and respond to these ideas. Both speeches are given by younger women focusing on contemporary perspectives; however, the lesson closes by looking back at our ancestors as scholars interview an elder in their communities. We (Kathryn and Jill) hope this juxtaposition leads to an analysis of the circular, cyclical, and forward movement of advocacy work.

"HeforShe" Speech—Emma Watson, United Nations

In 2014, Emma Watson, British actor and UN Women Goodwill Ambassador, co-hosted a special event for the UN Women's HeForShe campaign. The HeforShe campaign encourages men and boys to take up the issues of gender equality and equity as passionately as their women and girl counterparts. In this speech, Watson discusses how gender equality is everyone's issue and how gender stereotypes limit us all.

Listen to Watson's "HeforShe" Speech

Review Watson's speech—both the written transcript and video are available in our section appendix. After reviewing the speech, turn to a peer and discuss your reactions, reflections, and questions together.

- ◆ Which of her examples resonated with you?
- ◆ What would you challenge, refute, or qualify in this speech?
- ◆ What personal connections can you make to this speech?

"We Should All Be Feminists"—Chimamanda Adichie

Chimamanda Adichie, a Nigerian activist and author, gave a widely watched TED Talk called "We Should All Be Feminists." She later published a book under the same title. Explore this work by listening to her talk or reading the book or transcript version with your peers.

Discuss These Questions as a Class Community

◆ Which of Adichie's examples resonated with you?
◆ What would you challenge, refute, or qualify in this speech?
◆ What connections can you make to this speech?
◆ Compare and contrast Adichie and Watson's speeches about feminism.
◆ How is Adichie's definition similar or different from what you thought feminism meant?

A Feminist Lineage

Adichie (2014) said:

> My great grandmother, from the stories I've heard, was a feminist. She ran away from the house of the man she did not want to marry, and ended up marrying the man of her choice. She refused, she protested, she spoke up whenever she felt she's being deprived of access, of land, that sort of thing. My great grandmother did not know that word "feminist," but it doesn't mean that she wasn't one. More of us should reclaim that word.
>
> (p. 47–48)

Like Adichie's grandmother, many of our grandparents might not have called themselves feminists either, yet many engaged in important justice work that led to the opportunities their ancestors enjoy today. Below are a few examples to get you thinking:

◆ The great grandmother who escaped violence in her home country to start a new life in a place with more opportunities and safety for her children
◆ The great grandparents who stretched resources, sacrificed, and insisted that their daughter be the first in their family to attend college
◆ The great grandmother who wasn't able to attend school past sixth grade and who taught her children to read
◆ The great grandmother who joined a union to fight for equal pay after World War 2
◆ The grandparents who couldn't legally marry their partners of many decades (due to race, or sexuality, or both) and who taught their children about the power of love and hope
◆ The grandmother who raised dozens of children, including kin and foster youth, keeping young people safe and fed

- ◆ The grandparents who set up a community center or after school program that is still attended by youth today
- ◆ The grandmother who used her love of quilting to give hundreds of blankets to people experiencing homelessness in her city
- ◆ The grandmother who experienced housing and food insecurity in her youth and who now works in a health clinic addressing racial disparities in mental health

These elders are integral to your feminist lineage. Their sacrifice, values, convictions, and smarts are part of what brought you to this moment.

Gender Advocate Interview

The world you live in is different from the world your great grandmother lived in. Consider how your ancestors and those in the generations before you helped move the cause of justice forward. Brainstorm the names of gender advocates you know who are two to three generations older than you. You might think of family members or community members. You may be able to immediately think of someone in your life who protested against gender-based job discrimination, wrote justice articles for a local newspaper, provided shelter to someone leaving an abusive relationship, ran a soup kitchen for those experiencing food insecurity, welcomed refugees, or were the first in their family to step boldly into a new space. You may need some reflective space to think about who you want to interview and what stories of justice, advocacy, or survival you want to learn about through this assignment. Speaking with other family members may help point you to just the right person. You can also see an example interview in Unit 6, Lesson 2.

Gender Advocacy Is Expansive

Throughout this book, we (Kathryn and Jill) challenge scholars to consider how issues such as food insecurity, poverty, and infrastructure are essential feminist issues. The ways communities of color, Indigenous peoples, girls and women, and the LGBTQIA+ community are disproportionately affected by global issues, inequities, and structures are a critical lens for gender advocates to adopt as they seek ways to make a positive difference in their local and global communities.

Further, these lessons, and this activity, recognize that not all advocacy work is public or loud. Power and privilege directly impact the access people have to speak publicly or protest safely on behalf of issues that matter to them. This assignment celebrates that survival, love, and healing can all be critical acts of advocacy.

Brainstorm Interview Questions

Working with a partner, brainstorm some ideas about the types of questions you might want to ask during your interview. What does advocacy or justice mean to the person you interview? What memories or stories could they tell you? What changes in gender justice have they witnessed during their lifetime? What changes are they hoping for in the future? When you are brainstorming your ideas, write open-ended instead of closed-ended questions. For example, instead of asking, "Was it hard being a woman and owning your own business?" ask open-ended questions like, "What challenges did you face as a woman owning a business?" or "What are you most proud of as a woman who owns her own business?"

Conduct Your Interview

Decide how you are going to conduct your interview—a phone call, personal visit, over Zoom? When you conduct your interview, remember that you are there to listen and learn. Make eye contact; ask follow-up questions; and communicate, both verbally and nonverbally, that you are interested in what your interviewee is saying. It is also a good idea to take notes, and you may want to ask for permission to record the conversation. After you have conducted the interview, synthesize your notes by writing down the most interesting and important points you would like to share with your class about your conversation. Also consider how you will use the information you gained to be a gender advocate of your generation.

Presentation

Tell your classmates about your interview. Who is the person you interviewed? What are their most significant and inspiring contributions? What did you learn from them about advocacy and justice? End your presentation by sharing with your class how you will apply the lessons you learned in this interview to your own life.

⏸ Take a Reflective Beat

Reflect on you and your peers' presentations. What did they teach about the expansive nature of advocacy? How does this rich history inform our current work for a more just world?

Lesson 3: Feminisms Are for Everybody—Featured Scholar bell hooks

Teaching Notes

This lesson opens with an introductory text on differentiating feminisms. These distinctions are heady and academic. Review the text ahead of time to decide if its complexity is appropriate for your class. More advanced readers and those with some background in feminism already may want to read this text as is as a reading comprehension for discussion. Scholars for whom these concepts are brand new or those who have less experience with highly academic texts may benefit from a teacher summary of this information instead. If that is the case, share with your scholars the following key points:

1. Some scholars are moving away from the wave metaphor because it oversimplifies the feminist movements and may put generations against each other (e.g. my feminism is better than my mother's or grandmother's).
2. There are different frameworks within the feminist movement, including liberal feminisms, which work within systems to improve them; radical feminisms, which seek to create new systems that are more just; and Black feminisms, which explore the ways multiple identities and oppressions work together and which critique the ways racism has further marginalized communities of color even within feminist movements.

Feminisms—An Extremely Abridged Academic Introduction

Feminist movements, particularly in the United States, are often referenced in four waves. In brief, the first wave (1848–1920) is said to have focused on voting, property rights, and the abolition of slavery; the second wave (1960–1980) focused on equality, discrimination, and a rethinking of women's roles in both society and the home; the third wave (1990–2010) challenged assumptions of gender, sexuality, and beauty and complicated our understandings of identity and oppression through intersectionality; and the fourth wave (2010–present) utilizes the internet and media to advocate against sexual harassment and rape culture and for LGBTQIA+ rights, disability rights, and body positivity. While you will likely see references to these distinct waves in your reading, many scholars have moved away from this metaphor saying that it (1) discredits our global and historical movement toward equality as continuous and persistent, (2) positions the generations as against each other, and (3) oversimplifies the diversity of experiences that informed and continue to inform the movements for gender justice (Laughlin et al., 2010). For this reason, when we differentiate between feminisms in our lessons, we strive to do so by their unique theoretical, historical, and cultural contexts that are often overlapping and sometimes in conversation, conflict, or cooperation with each other.

Term	Definition
Liberal feminisms	A framework that operates *within* systems to improve them. Cornerstones of this framework include working toward equal opportunity, access, individual rights, liberty, and legislative equity (Fishman-Weaver, 2017). Establishing better sexual harassment or equal opportunity hiring practices are examples of initiatives that liberal feminists might advocate for.
Radical feminisms	A framework that operates *beyond* systems to construct new structures and possibilities. Radical feminists believe that our systems are so deeply rooted in inequity and oppression they must be fundamentally deconstructed, reimagined, and built anew. A famous radical feminist text is Audre Lorde's essay "The Master's Tools Will Never Dismantle the Master's House" (2015).
Black feminisms	This framework centers the experiences of Black women while exploring the ways multiple identities and oppressions intersect to create contextualized experiences and conditions within systems. Black feminisms work concurrently on eradicating racism and sexism in the work toward a more just world. (See especially Sojourner Truth, Kimberlé Crenshaw, Angela Davis, and bell hooks.)
Queer theory	A critical framework that challenges power dynamics related to gender and sexuality. Queer theory rejects essentialist (or pre-determined) definitions and binary thinking. Rather than assuming that categories of gender, sex, and sexuality are natural and fixed, queer theorists seek a more nuanced understanding of gender as dynamic and negotiated. This framework celebrates a full spectrum of identities. Queer theory frameworks are used in literary criticism, political criticism, sociology studies, and more layered accounts of history. (See especially Gloria Anzaldúa, Adrienne Rich, Judith Butler, and Eve Kosofsky Sedgwick.)

bell hooks—Foundations of Knowledge

These frameworks and ideologies shape how you view the world and the approaches you take toward bringing about positive change. In the next section of this lesson, you will explore your own beliefs about knowledge production through the work of bell hooks, a thought leader in *Black feminisms*.

Gloria Jean Watkins (1952–2021) published under the pseudonym bell hooks. This name honored her maternal great grandmother. hooks used a lowercase version of the name to emphasize that the focus is on the work, not the person. A prolific author and feminist scholar, bell hooks' work explores race, class, gender, identity, education, and critical consciousness.

hooks proudly identified as a Black, queer feminist scholar. Her work encouraged love, healing, and finding new ways to live and come together. These beliefs were grounded in her queer identity. hooks defined queerness as "the self that is at odds with everything around it and has to invent and create and find a place to speak and to thrive and to live" (Ibrahim, 2021, para 3). In 1983 (republished in 2014), she wrote *Feminist Theory: From Margin to Center*, which called on scholars and activists to engage in feminism that recognized the ways racism, classism, and sexism worked as cooperative webs of oppression. Her vision for justice is one that ends sexist exploitation and oppression while working with the same diligence to end other systems of oppression including racism (hooks, 2014).

Term	Definition
Critical consciousness	An ability to see and understand inequities in our communities and a commitment to take action against injustices.
Patriarchy	A system of government, society, or family in which men hold power and women are systematically excluded from power. Feminist movements seek to dismantle patriarchal systems and establish more equitable systems.

Scholarly Connections

 Thought Questions

◆ Where did you learn about gender, inclusion, and sexism?
◆ Were these concepts that someone specifically taught you, or were they things you picked up on through your lived experiences?

In the next activity, you will have the opportunity to think deeply about gender and advocacy work. Read and respond to the quotes from Chapter 4 of bell hooks' book *Feminism Is for Everybody* (2020). This chapter outlines some of hooks' ideology about education and critical consciousness.

◆ What have you learned about gender, sexism, discrimination, and equality from your families and other spaces like school, faith communities, and sports?

◆ How have you or other people you know been taught to accept sexist thinking? What does that look like?

◆ What does the media teach young people about gender and feminism? Are those lessons positive, negative, or a combination of both? How so?

◆ Why is work with young people so important?

◆ What work can young people do to resist discrimination and sexism?

"Most of us had been socialized by parents and society to accept sexist thinking. We had not taken time to figure out the roots of our perceptions." (p. 19)

"By failing to create a mass-based educational movement to teach everyone about feminism we allow mainstream patriarchal mass media to remain the primary place where folks learn about feminism, and most of what they learn is negative." (p. 23)

"We need work that is especially geared towards youth culture. No one produces this work in academic settings." (p. 23)

Concept Synthesis Project—WGST & Me

Name_____ Date_____

Over the last two units, you have started to learn about the breadth of Women's and Gender Studies as well as different feminist frameworks. Depending on how your class community organized your learning, you may have completed several or all the following activities:

Activating Prior Knowledge—Feminist T-Shirt Design
UNIT 1: Feminist Theory—Introduction
Lesson 1: SDG 5—Target Research
Lesson 2: Start Where You Are—Thought Work on WGST and Feminism
Lesson 3: Scholar Study—Sojourner Truth
UNIT 2: We Can All Be Changemakers for Justice
Lesson 1: Gender-Expansive Identity Readings
Lesson 2: Feminist Speech Analysis (Emma Watson and Chimamanda Adichie)
Lesson 3: Feminisms and Critical Consciousness Thought Work (bell hooks)

Take some time to go through your own growing body of Women's and Gender Studies work. Look for trends, areas for further exploration, and ideas you are proud of.

You Have Important Things to Say
- ◆ What issues are you drawn to?
- ◆ What questions do you want to explore next?
- ◆ What scholars, leaders, and frameworks did you resonate with?

As we close out these units, synthesize your own growing framework for gender advocacy into a culminating project. Choose one of the following prompts and craft a thoughtful response. Your response may build directly on one of the activities you started in this unit, or it may be a completely new product.

Synthesis Prompts
- ◆ How can young people persist in the fight for justice, representation, equity, and inclusion? Give specific local and global examples.

Used with permission from Fishman-Weaver and Clingan, Teaching Women's and Gender Studies. Copyright © 2023, Taylor and Francis, Inc.

◆ What are the differences between equality and equity? How do these concepts relate to our work as Women's and Gender Studies scholars?
◆ Identify local organizations in your communities who are doing important advocacy work around issues of gender, representation, and inclusion? How can you support these efforts?

Present your response in a poster, essay, skit, mini-documentary, or editorial. Below are some guidelines to consider as you work on your synthesis project.

Title and medium	What is the title of your work? What is the meaning of that title? In this project, you have the creative latitude to use any kind of medium you want (e.g. music, art, videography, essay writing, etc.). Why did you choose the medium you did?
Thesis	What is the main message of your project? What do you want readers or viewers to learn or experience when they read or see your work?
Feminist theory	How does your project connect to one or more of the feminist theories or key vocabulary we learned in these units? What ideas are you building on or illustrating? Note: When you draw on another scholar's work, it is important to give them credit by citing their work.
Course theme(s)	How does your project illustrate or show a commitment to resistance, representation, or radical hope? Be specific.
Inspiration	Whose shoulders are you standing on? How have your own lived experiences contributed to the issues you are reporting on and care about?

Used with permission from Fishman-Weaver and Clingan, Teaching Women's and Gender Studies. Copyright © 2023, Taylor and Francis, Inc.

Extension Exercises for Concept 1

Deconstructing the Gender Box—Creative Challenge

The gender box is a metaphor often used to illustrate the ways binary thinking limits identity and behavior.

Term	Definition
Gender box	Gender roles that are prescribed or constructed by society.
Binary thinking	Believing there are only two possibilities.

Think about a more inclusive visual of gender than a box and create an artistic representation of what that might look like. Some ideas are amorphous shapes, Venn diagrams, and spectrums. Because you are literally *thinking outside the box* here, feel free to come up with your own creative ideas!

◆ What expansive possibilities did you most resonate within thinking through this activity?
◆ How can you take this activity from an art or thinking task to action and application?

Children's Book

Create a children's book that explains Women's and Gender Studies in a way that elementary-aged children would understand. Another idea is to create a children's book of one of the key figures or pivotal moments in feminist history.

Snap Interview

Do snap interviews with ten people asking these questions:

◆ How would you define Women's and Gender Studies?
◆ How would you define feminism?
◆ What are feminist accomplishments from the past 100 years?
◆ Are you a feminist? Why or why not?

A Mantra for Moving Past Imposter Syndrome

Toward the end of her speech to the United Nations, Emma Watson references a common feeling called *imposter syndrome*.

Term	Definition
Imposter syndrome	A feeling or belief that you aren't qualified for the tasks you have been asked to do.

She also commits to moving forward even as she wonders if she is the right person for the task. "If not me, who, if not now, when . . . I don't know if I am qualified to be here. All I know is that I care about this problem. And I want to make it better" (United Nations, 2014).

Imposter syndrome is common and can happen anywhere. You might experience it in class, on the field, in your extracurriculars, or anywhere you are called to do something challenging or just out of your comfort zone. Recognizing and normalizing imposter syndrome can be a source of strength. While imposter syndrome can feel deeply personal, it is also important to look at these feelings through some of the lenses introduced in these lessons. Often feelings of imposter syndrome are triggered by racism, classism, sexism, and homophobia. Continued work toward justice and equity is essential in cultivating spaces that are inclusive and brave.

Throughout these units, you will be asked to identify issues you care deeply about, to advocate to make your communities more just and inclusive, and to share personal stories. All of these tasks require courage. As you practice bravery and navigate the big feelings that come with doing courageous tasks, it may help to have some language and strategies for addressing imposter syndrome.

Think about an area in your life where you feel or have felt imposter syndrome. Try this mantra and keep it in mind whenever you need a little boost.

"If not me, who, if not now, when. I belong in this

_____

(class/activity/leadership role)

I care about _____. And can do this."
(why you are in this class/activity/role)

Key Figures

In our "Beyond the Binary" lesson, scholars learn more about the kathoey, the hijra, and two-spirit people. However, the lessons do not go into depth into specific key figures. As an extension, identify and research a key figure from any of these identity groups. The links in our chapter appendix offer a helpful starting place.

Helpful Links

- Sojourner Truth's "Ain't I a Woman?" speech available on Learning for Justice: www.learningforjustice.org/classroom-resources/texts/aint-i-a-woman
- *The New York Times*: The Peculiar Position of India's Third Gender (note this article discusses sex work): www.nytimes.com/2018/02/17/style/india-third-gender-hijras-transgender.html
- 12 Incredible Indigenous LGBTQ Women and Two-Spirit People You Should Know: www.autostraddle.com/12-awesome-native-american-and-first-nation-lgbtq-women-and-two-spirit-people-311473/
- Emma Watson's HeforShe Speech—Video: www.youtube.com/watch?v=gkjW9PZBRfk
- Emma Watson's "HeforShe" Speech—Transcript: www.unwomen.org/en/news/stories/2014/9/emma-watson-gender-equality-is-your-issue-too
- HeforShe Alliance web page: www.heforshe.org/en
- Chimamanda Adichie—"We Should All Be Feminists": www.ted.com/talks/chimamanda_ngozi_adichie_we_should_all_be_feminists
- Kamala Harris Acceptance Speech: www.youtube.com/watch?v=-ExPm_hJQYpQ
- 7 Historic Firsts that Prove Representation Matters in Politics https://www.wellandgood.com/representation-in-politics/

Notes

[1] While the focus quote belongs to one bright young person, out of respect for their identity and privacy, "Mae" is a composite of a few different young people I've worked and learned with.

[2] If scholars would like some help getting started, we have provided an example chart in the chapter I don't see this example in the appendix?

[3] Recognizing these limitations, we (Kathryn and Jill) worked specifically with scholars more familiar with the cultural backgrounds of India and Thailand on this lesson.

Art, Emotion, and Resistance

**Prefácio do capítulo por
Stefani Domingues,
Consultora Editorial**

Stefani Domingues (ela/dela) tem 28 anos e é orgulhosamente latina, feminista, educadora e mobilizadora de juventudes. Ela é formada em Psicologia e atualmente atua como Psicóloga Clínica para adolescentes e mulheres jovens. Antes disso, ela trabalhou por cinco anos com alunos do ensino fundamental e médio que buscavam educação internacional. Stefani acredita que as meninas podem ganhar confiança inspirando-se em mulheres fortes e talentosas que vieram antes de nós. Em seu tempo livre, ela gosta de ler romances e sua autora favorita é a escritora brasileira Clarice Lispector. Como um sonho pessoal, Stefani deseja um dia publicar seu próprio romance sobre uma protagonista feminina ousada.

**Foreword by
Stefani Domingues,
Advisory Editor**

Stefani Domingues (she/her) is 28 years old and is a proud Latina, feminist, educator, and youth mobilizer. She holds a bachelor's degree in psychology and currently serves as clinical psychologist for adolescents and young women. Prior to that, she worked for five years serving middle and high school students who were pursuing international education. Stefani believes that young girls can gain confidence by relating to strong and talented women who came before them. In her free time, she enjoys reading novels. Her favorite author is the Brazilian writer Clarice Lispector. As a personal dream, Stefani wishes to someday publish her own novel featuring a bold feminine protagonist.

DOI: 10.4324/9781003289500-3

Sou orgulhosamente latina, feminista, educadora e mobilizadora de joventudes. Nos últimos 5 anos, trabalhei com educação internacional para alunas e alunos do Ensino Fundamental e Médio. Atualmente atuo como psicóloga clínica de meninas e mulheres jovens. Na prática clínica, juntas, construímos um ambiente seguro para compartilhar lutas, sucessos e criar modos de usar as emoções de forma poderosa e transformadora.

Durante minha adolescência, me vi procurando em todos os lugares por representação e inspiração femininas. Não foi até recentemente que eu entendi o porquê de precisar procurar tanto. Percebi que era mais difícil me imaginar em lugares protagonistas simplesmente porque não estava acostumada a ver mulheres em cargos de liderança, ou ter sua arte celebrada em galerias, ou viver uma história que não fosse sobretudo sobre casamento ou maternidade. As formas como as mulheres são representadas ou não são importantes para mim e para as jovens com quem trabalho. Ao ver apenas uma história ou uma versão dela, parecia que o casamento e a maternidade não eram escolhas, mas a única conquista pela qual eu deveria me esforçar ou me orgulhar. Eu buscava ansiosamente por uma maior representação de gênero e só conseguia encontrá-la quando procurava ativamente por isso.

Exatamente por isso que este livro, *Teaching Women's e Gender Studies*, é tão importante. Ele propõe preencher uma lacuna e engajar as gerações mais jovens na construção de uma sociedade mais justa. A fim de capacitar os jovens e alcançar equidade de gênero, alunas e alunos precisam ser intencionalmente introduzidos aos estudos de gênero e teorias feministas.

I am a proud Latina, feminist, educator, and youth mobilizer. For the past five years, I've worked with international education for middle and high school students. Currently, I serve as a clinical psychologist for girls and young women. In private practice, together, we build a safe environment to share struggles and successes and create ways to use our emotions in a powerful and transformative way.

Growing up, I found myself looking everywhere for women's representation and inspiration. It was not until recently that I understood why. I realized that it was harder for me to picture myself in protagonistic places simply because I was not used to seeing women in leadership positions, having their art celebrated in galleries, or living a story that was not primarily about marriage or motherhood. The ways women are represented or not represented mattered to me, and it matters to the young people I work with. By only seeing one story or one version of a story, it seemed that marriage and motherhood were not choices, but the only achievement I should strive for or be proud of. I was eager for greater gender representation, and I could only find it when I was actively looking for it.

That is why this resource, *Teaching Women's and Gender Studies*, is so important. It proposes to fill a gap and engage young generations in building a more equitable society. To empower young people and achieve gender justice, students need to be intentionally introduced to gender studies and feminist theories.

Cada um de nós lê a partir de seu próprio contexto e experiências vividas. Enquanto trabalhava com Kathryn e Jill neste capítulo, muitas vezes pensei na cantora brasileira Elza Soares (1930–2022) que cantou *"minha voz uso pra dizer o que se cala."* Nascida no Brasil, sua voz foi um instrumento de resistência que inspirou a muitas, inclusive a mim. Sua arte explorou a violência e as desigualdades que a acompanharam ao longo de sua vida; no entanto, ao ouvir suas músicas, você também pode ouvir sua alegria, raiva e criatividade.

Em "Concept 4: Art, Emotion and Resistance" as autoras afirmam que a arte é um instrumento de resistência. Leitores entenderão como a alegria pode levar à ação, como a raiva pode criar beleza e como a criatividade pode ser uma chave essencial de combate às injustiças sociais.

Kathryn e Jill afetivamente conduzem estudantes e educadores por uma exposição de pintoras, escritoras e poetizas engajadas no trabalho feminista. Essas obras e diversos exemplos podem inspirar a juventude a entender como as artes podem levar à transformação. Professores, estudantes e educadores encontrarão recursos poderosos para promover discussões importantes em sala de aula. Conhecerão também mulheres de destaque, artistas pretas e latinas que impactaram suas comunidades. Através deste trabalho, você e suas salas de aula também podem resistir à injustiça e encontrar uma esperança radical.

Each of us reads from our own context and lived experiences. As I was working with Kathryn and Jill on this section, I often thought of the Brazilian singer Elza Soares (1930–2022). She sang that *"minha voz eu uso pra dizer o que se cala.*[1]*"* Growing up in Brazil, her voice was an instrument for resistance that inspired my peers and me. Her art explored the violence and inequalities that accompanied her throughout her life; however, when listening to her songs, you can also hear joy, anger, and creativity.

In "Concept 4: Art, Emotion and Resistance," the authors state that *art is an instrument for resistance.* Readers will understand how joy can lead to action, how anger can create beauty, and how creativity can be an essential key to fight social injustices.

Kathryn and Jill affectionately walk scholars and educators through an exhibition of painters, writers, and poets engaged in feminist work. These works and diverse examples can inspire youth to see how the arts can lead to transformation. Teachers, scholars, and educators will find powerful resources to promote important discussions in the classroom. They will also meet outstanding women, Black, and Latin artists who impacted their communities. Through this work, you and your class communities can seek ways to resist injustice and find radical hope.

Teaching Concept Overview—Art, Emotion, and Resistance

Purpose: These two units center joy, creativity, and critique. They affirm that all emotions are valid and that art, anger, and joy can be powerful forms of resistance. Drawing on social science and art traditions from around the world, these units invite scholars to examine the material conditions and everyday experiences of their lives as sites for justice, beauty, and possibility. Building on the work of artists, activists, and social scientists, Unit 3 introduces scholars to bold ideas about emotion, resistance, and justice. In Unit 4, scholars begin or create many different creative and art works. This section culminates with bringing one of these art pieces to completion. These synthesis art projects expound on one of our book themes—*resistance, representation*, and *radical hope*—and explore the connections between emotion and change.

✔ Objectives

By the end of these units, scholars will be able to:

- ◆ Define *affective development*.
- ◆ Explain connections between social emotional learning and racial justice.
- ◆ Share more about the advocacy work of Malala Yousafszai.
- ◆ Explore the ways anger and joy can be acts of resistance.
- ◆ Analyze several works of art across mediums and cultures including Shamsia Hassani's street art, Christine ("CK") Sun Kim, and the *MaestraPeace* mural in San Francisco, CA.

❓ Essential Questions for Scholars

- ◆ What does it look like to claim your emotions and use them to advance justice and inclusion?
- ◆ How is art a vehicle for positive change?
- ◆ Is joy a fundamental human right? If so, how can we affirm it for all?

🕤 Reflective Questions for Educators

- ◆ How can I cultivate affective and arts education in my classes?
- ◆ How can I add more joy to my teaching and curriculum?

Activate Prior Knowledge—Afrobubblegum	
Unit 3—Affective Development: In More Voices	**Unit 4—Art as Resistance**

Lesson 1—In More Voices: Affective Development and SEL Lesson 2—One Child . . . Can Change the World Lesson 3—Audre Lorde: "The Uses of Anger"	Lesson 1—Feminist Art Movement Lesson 2—*MaestraPeace*: San Francisco Women's Mural Lesson 3—Shamsia Hassani: Street Art as Resistance Lesson 4—Christine ("CK") Sun Kim, Sound Artist
Synthesis: Art Project—Emotion and Resistance	

Concept Dedications

Kathryn's Dedication—I dedicate this section to the truth tellers in my action research class. Over the summer of 2015, I taught an action research class for rising high school juniors. The scholars in my class spent their summer researching personal truths. In particular, their project aimed to shine a light on truths that are difficult to hold and difficult to share. As you might imagine, this was a heart-heavy project. It also taught me some of the most important lessons I've ever learned about supporting young people as they navigate the celebrations and tribulations of adolescence.

In addition to receiving and coding nearly 100 stories, my scholars sought specific ways to wrap their peers in care. These included sharing resources on mental health, eating disorders, healthy relationships, LGBTQIA+ inclusion, and racial justice. They presented their research in a closing ceremony.

When asked, the scholars shared the two most important things they learned were (1) that everyone is navigating more than they share and (2) that no matter what is happening, you are not alone. On my best days, these lessons have transformed the way I teach, parent, and exist as a human being. Their final presentation left our entire school in tears and ended in a lengthy standing ovation. Young people not only can change the world; they already are.

Jill's Dedication—When my daughter was young, I taught the courses Introduction to Literature and The Short Story in the Continuing Education Department at the nearby university where I had graduated with my master's degree. My classes were super tiny, and I was paid by the student, so I (maybe) broke even on the cost of child care, but I absolutely loved teaching these students. The classes took place in the evenings, and my students, who had spent long days in an office or factory or construction site or at home with their children, showed up in my classroom with such grace and presence, eager to learn and discuss and debate and create.

What I remember most about these students is how they, with their layered life experiences, brought the art of literature to life for me in ways I hadn't quite experienced before. When I think about these evenings, I don't picture myself standing behind a podium lecturing; instead, I picture myself perched on the edge of a desk listening. I will never forget not quite grasping a student's intense connection to Tillie Olsen's "I Stand Here Ironing" but feeling swept into her passion even if I couldn't (yet) articulate that passion along with her. I will never forget the student who saw art in math and who connected to the intersections of identity, mental health, and equations in David Auburn's play *Proof*. I will never forget how, even with their full, busy lives, they creatively and energetically connected to stories of injustice and justice and how those stories inspired them to both create and advocate.

Those classes, with those students, showed me how art and creativity and lived experiences could all thread together into a rich tapestry that was woven with the intricate threads of justice and bright with the patterns of hope. I dedicate this chapter to those thinkers and writers and creators, and I am grateful for how they shape my perspectives even today.

Concept Introduction by Kathryn and Jill

One year, Jill and I (Kathryn) wrote to our colleagues:

> We love Women's History Month and each year we were happy that it has arrived again! This happiness is, of course, both complicated and incomplete. As we consider the narrative arc of women's history, it is not always (or even often) a happy history. The complex history and activism that has brought us to today includes violence, discrimination, exclusion, and fear. However, it also includes resistance, hope, and yes, tremendous moments of joy.

Like anger, joy is a powerful emotion that can drive both creation and connection. In these units, we extend that idea by suggesting that joy is a universal human right and that affirming this right for girls and women is a worthwhile feminist endeavor. In these lessons, scholars learn about artists, authors, activists, and social scientists contributing to our knowledge of emotions, social experiences, and the power of new perspectives. With a focus on affective education and close reading, these lessons support young people as they claim or reclaim their emotions (including their biggest and messiest feelings) as valid and important. We hope to challenge scholars (and educators) to consider how joy, anger, and creation can all be powerful vehicles for positive change.

Teaching Notes—Opportunities to Collaborate

These lessons offer many opportunities for collaboration with educators in your school and surrounding communities. School counselors, psychologists, and therapists can be important guest experts and facilitators for conversations around affective development, emotional regulation, belonging, and social emotional learning. Further, art educators and local artists can add wisdom to our work around creating art, analyzing art, and using art as a tool for resistance. Community-based spaces in your schools or neighborhoods can serve as sites for galleries and exhibits for the synthesis projects.

Educator Letter for Concept 2—*In All Its Nuances*

Dear Valued Educator,

In this connecting space, we (Kathryn and Jill) invite you to think with us about the upcoming chapter content. Let's sit down with a blank canvas and some paints as we settle in together to think about these units on emotion, affective development, and the power of art. Like the young people we learn with, these units are vibrant and complex. These also aren't units Jill and I (Kathryn) could have written in our first years in the classroom. For both of us, there are experiences we have had and people (including young people) who have changed us and made us ready for this content. As always, we want to keep reminding you that your work matters, and, of course, we want to talk about what care might look like **for you** in teaching these lessons.

Your Work Matters

These lessons affirm your scholars' emotions and lived experiences. They declare that all experiences and feelings are valid and important. These activities celebrate representation, resistance, and the creative power of the arts. They invite scholars to use multiple mediums to express their feelings, passions, and stories. As scholars engage in creative works from around the world, we (Kathryn and Jill) hope they find new points of entry for extraordinary and ordinary conversations about justice, equity, and belonging.

Care Strategies for Educators

◆ **Sphere of influence**—As an educator, you have a vast sphere of influence; however, that sphere is not limitless. As you and your scholars explore big emotions, global challenges, and difficult stories, it may help to reflect on what you can control and let go of some of what you can't control. For example, you can control how affirmed and seen young people feel in your classroom, but you can't control the things that happened to them when they were younger. You can control how you and your class choose to show up for refugees and welcome new neighbors to your communities; however, you can't control the armed conflicts that already contributed to many of our refugee crises. You can control how you affirm feelings when a young person shares their story, but you can't control what feelings that story brings up for them. Recognizing what is within your sphere of influence and committing to making those choices with humanity, dignity, and compassion is noble work. Recognizing what is outside of your sphere of influence makes this work more tenable.

◆ **Resist the need to tie everything up with a bow**—The same program where I (Kathryn) worked with the truth tellers (see pp. 65) had a school norm that said, "Expect unfinished business." This norm helped us all resist the urge to tie everything up with a bow. We knew that in our classes we would tackle difficult topics and big lessons, and we knew at the end of class, the unit, or even the whole program, not everything would be solved or resolved. Giving ourselves permission to dare boldly, to work through complicated concepts, and then to be at peace with the fact that the work continues well beyond this class and this semester, let us take risks, launch new projects, and learn outside our comfort zones.

◆ **Embrace the power of creating**—The lessons in Unit 4 celebrate the power of the arts as a tool for expression, resistance, and social justice. Creating, crafting, and arts have always been tools to make sense of the world, to explore beauty, and to invite creative thinking.

The American Art Therapy Association (2017) writes that art and art therapy "engages the mind, body, and spirit in ways that are distinct from verbal articulation alone. . . . Visual and symbolic expression gives voice to experience, and empowers individual, communal, and societal transformation" (para 7).

In these lessons, we (Kathryn and Jill) encourage you to cultivate space for your scholars to create art. However, we also want to encourage and invite you to create art alongside your scholars. At the beginning of this letter, we shared that we were inviting you to join us at a table with canvases and paints; we could have also said with magazines and glue. As a care strategy, it doesn't matter what materials you use or even what your final product looks like. Whether you draw, paint, doodle, collage, or create, your voice in all its nuances matters.

With admiration,

Kathryn and Jill

Activate Prior Knowledge—Afrobubblegum

Teaching Notes

If it is appropriate for your school context, distribute big pieces of bright pink bubblegum and turn on some happy music as scholars work through the Afrobubblegum questions. This is a lesson about joy. Joy matters. In these opening activities, you will introduce scholars to Wanuri Kaihu as they consider the important and multifaceted role joy plays in our lives and our art.

Before we engage in this study, how are you holding space for joy? This might sound like an odd question, particularly in the context of global crises.

However, what if I (Kathryn) encouraged you not to think of joy and injustice as mutually exclusive? What if, in fact, joy and art could be powerful forms of resistance and imagination? Throughout this book, we (Kathryn and Jill) hope to offer more complete histories; however, we also want to caution against teaching only stories of despair, struggle, and injustice. These kinds of stories perpetuate what social scientist and Indigenous scholar Eve Tuck calls "damage-centered frameworks" (2009). Inclusive teaching should disrupt this narrative.

Here are three considerations as you engage in the joyful celebration of affirming humanity, practicing inclusion, and teaching more complete stories:

- ◆ Seek every opportunity to affirm and celebrate your scholars, particularly those who may have had limited mirror books and resources in schools.
- ◆ Ask yourself whose stories are being told in your curriculum and how they are being told.
- ◆ Ask yourself what a *joy audit* might look like in your classes. If you were to take a reflective beat at the end of each class period, could you point to specific moments of joy?

Thought Questions

◆ What does the term Afrobubblegum make you think of?
◆ How does this phrase make you feel?
◆ Sketch your feelings about this term.

Wanuri Kahiu, the founder of Afrobubblegum, is a Kenyan film producer, artist, and advocate. She strives to create art that is delightful and showcases joyful stories from Africa. She describes the Afrobubblegum movement in this way:

> We believe in a fun, fierce and frivolous representation of Africa. To that end, we work to curate, commission and create fun work that celebrates joy. We are storytellers, clothes makers, graphic designers, musicians, lovers of life, joy harbingers, beauty mongers, hope sayers.
> (Afrobubblegum, n.d., para 1–2)

In her TED Talk "Fun, fierce and fantastical African art," Kahiu (2017) expresses the concern that there is still *a single story of Africa*[2] and that this story is too often void of joy. Her work strives to offer a different story, one that is *fun, fierce, and frivolous.* She asserts that fun is political because it changes the narrative. If Kahiu tells stories of African people who are "loving and thriving and living a beautiful, vibrant life," it flips the script of the African narrative being a single story of suffering. That story becomes, instead, one about *shared humanity* through *shared joy.* Telling this sort of story not only layers the African narrative with joy and a shared humanity for those who read and witness it, but it also layers that same joyful story for Africans who are living it. Kahiu captures and represents this joy in her stories about "futuristic girls that risk everything to save plants or to race camels or even just to dance to honor fun" (para 6).

Mikela Henry-Lowe is a contemporary Jamaican artist based in London. Like Kahiu, her work aims to celebrate a more joyful representation of Black women. Known for her bold use of color and pattern, Henry-Lowe's portraits offer powerful and more complete stories of Black womanhood. In an interview, Henry-Lowe was asked, "What knowledge do you hope people walk away with after seeing your work?" Her answer, "That Black women are beautiful, that Black women aren't only the stereotypes placed upon them by society. I want all types of beauty to be celebrated. It's all about positivity" (Woodson, 2020, para 8–9).

View several of Henry-Lowe's portraits.[3] After viewing the images and discussing Kahiu's mission, discuss these questions on representation and joy.

 Thought Questions

- ◆ Do you agree that fun can be political?
- ◆ Can joy have a mission?
- ◆ How do beautiful and joyful images help tell more complete stories?
- ◆ How does joy apply to our work around representation, resistance, and radical hope?

Over the next two units, you will explore the connections among art, emotion, and resistance. You will explore art, affective development, representation, and the power of imagination. While engaging in this work—or any work—it helps to keep a joyful song in your pocket. In this next activity, you and your classmates will create an individualized joy playlist.

Create a Joy Playlist

Brainstorm a list of songs that bring you immeasurable joy, songs you can't help but dance to, songs that remind you of happy times, and songs that can take a rough patch and make it a little brighter.

Feeling a bit more poetic? Your playlist can also include sounds, people, or even sights that make you chuckle with delight, connection, or genuine happiness.

Consider your playlist. What does it say about you, and how can you use it to bring joy and purpose to your days?

Exit Question: Is joy a fundamental human right? If so, how can we affirm it for all?

Unit 3—Affective Development: In More Voices

These lessons ask scholars to think critically about the emotional domain and the power of their own feelings. Much of the early publications and funded research on affective development, which studies "the capacity to experience, express, and interpret the full range of emotions and . . . the ability to cope with them appropriately" (*APA Dictionary of Psychology*, n.d.), was conducted by men. However, beginning in the 1980s, feminist scholars began publishing powerful critiques and new work in this area. Scholars and educators also expanded the focus from affective development to include affective education as well. Through affective education, scholars learn about emotional regulation; goal setting; the relationship between feeling, thinking, and acting; belonging and relationships; and self-efficacy. These topics are directly related to the scholarship on gender, power, and social constructs.

In the following unit, scholars will explore Dena Simmons' and Carol Gilligan's work, which opened up discussions to more voices in general and to the voices of Black, Indigenous, and people of color and women in particular. Then building on the extraordinary example of Malala Yousafzai, a young woman who used her passions to change the world, scholars will consider how they too, can leverage their passions for social good. The unit closes with an analysis of Audre Lorde's essay on the uses of anger. We (Kathryn and Jill) hope scholars leave this lesson knowing that their feelings are valid and powerful, that joy and anger can be forms of resistance and that in the words of Yousafzai "One child, one book, one teacher, one pen, can change the world" (United Nations, 2013, 16:36).

Teaching Notes

Gloria Ladson-Billings (2021), the seminal scholar on culturally relevant pedagogies, reminds us that

> Culturally relevant/sustaining/revitalizing/reality pedagogies is designed to cultivate students' voices, entrepreneurial inclinations, and inventive spirits . . . these pedagogies seek to open up worlds of possibilities for each student to bring [their] whole self into the classroom and into the world
>
> (p. 354)

As you *open up worlds of possibilities*, honor genius, and create space for new questions, your classes will also engage in critical perspectives about systems and constructs. For example, in these lessons, scholars may

---

wrestle with the messages they receive about feelings, including what emotions they should have or express and to what extent these should be expressed. As you introduce affective education into your classrooms, you may enter into new and important conversations around agency and belonging (Fishman-Weaver, 2018). This work is only possible within spaces that have a clear and unequivocal commitment to culturally relevant (Ladson-Billings, 2021) and antiracist teaching methods. In her work on racial trauma and social emotional learning (SEL), Dr. Donna Ford (2020) discusses how this emotional work must center the lived experiences of all students in ways that are both culturally responsive and sustaining (see Paris Django's work).

> Racial trauma is prevalent but students of color cannot be helped with SEL prevention and intervention methods that in any way ignore and discount how both culture-blindness and cultural assaults dehumanize people of color; these illustrate how both are antithetical to *everything* that SEL stands for in principle and practice.
>
> (Ford, 2020, para 10)

This unit—and book—is written with a feminist resolve to affirm the rights of young people to experience a full range of emotions, including big and complex feelings like joy and anger, and to live safely and boldly as their authentic selves.

Key Term: *Authenticity*

In these units, *authenticity* refers to practices that honor all lived experiences as valid and affirm the cultural wisdom and complexities each member of our school community brings to the classroom. People are complex and multifaceted. Leaning into authenticity means honoring those many facets and complexities, including identities, experiences, values, culture, personality, passions, and emotions. Authenticity is a journey. It is a process of honestly learning, experiencing, questioning, listening, thinking, and creating your own story while also participating in the authentic stories of others.

Lesson 1: In More Voices—Affective Development and SEL

Term	Definition
Social emotional learning (SEL)	Teaching and learning that is focused on health, connection, and care. SEL includes learning about emotions, identities, healthy relationships, attitudes and mindsets, empathy, and decision making.
Affective development	The capacity to recognize, experience, and express a broad range of emotions and the ability to respond well to the emotions and emotional cues of others. Affective development is a process that happens over time as people learn more about their emotional state, emotional regulation, and strategies to navigate our social world.
Strengths-based approaches	Also known as *asset-based approaches*, these represent a commitment to focus on strengths, assets, talents, and genius. Key questions include: What is going well? What are my or my community's strengths? • The opposite of strengths-based approaches are *deficit-based approaches*.

This lesson asks you to commit to listening and including more voices in the conversation and research around affective development and SEL. In whose voices? Dr. Carol Gilligan, who advocated for greater gender representation and understanding in the research on affective development, and Dr. Dena Simmons' work are about expanding our understanding of how racial justice and SEL can (and must!) work together.

 Thought Question

Is SEL something you can achieve or something you must always keep striving toward?

- ◆ If it is something you can achieve, how will you know when you've done so?
- ◆ If it is something you must always keep learning, how do you know you're making progress? How can you stay motivated?

Dr. Dena Simmons—LiberatED

Just like racial justice and healing, Dr. Dena Simmons (2021) writes that SEL is also a process. Dr. Simmons is an educator, researcher, and racial justice advocate. She believes it is important to look at justice, wellness, and persistence as a continuous commitment to improvement. That is, wellness isn't something you can achieve but is something you can improve on.

Dr. Simmons's work focuses on the intersection of SEL and racial justice. She has done this work at Yale and now in her own collective, LiberatED. However, before working in these spaces, she honed her learning as a middle school teacher. This activity builds on one of her classroom activities on strengths-based learning and identity.

Strengths-Based Approaches—H x 4

The following activity takes an asset-based approach to identity. You will create a strengths-based H x 4 poster on your hands, head, heart, and home. As always, creativity is encouraged. After you have had time to work on your posters, present and display them in the classroom.

Hands	Talents in doing	What do I love to do? What do I do well?
Head	Talents in thinking	What is something I am an expert in? What is something I am proud to be learning about?
Heart	Passions and interests	What lights me up? What issues do I care deeply about?
Home	Belonging in my community	What does home mean to me? What places are important or meaningful to me?

Adapted from D. Simmons (2012)

Carol Gilligan—In a Different Voice

Carol Gilligan worked as a research assistant for Lawrence Kohlberg. While both scholars worked on affective development, Gilligan criticized Kohlberg's belief that moral development could be explained with predictable patterns. She said that such an understanding was too simple and that emotions and ethical development are not always objective, reasoned, and rational. Instead, Gilligan suggested that there is "a different voice" to our moral/emotional development. This voice, which she calls "an ethics of care" (Webteam, 2011, para 2), includes making moral decisions based on historical context and relationships. Gilligan's critique of Kohlberg, *In a Different Voice* (1982), was published to much acclaim. This work opened up new conversations about psychological and moral development, gendered differences in emotional development, and Gilligan's career studying affective development for women and girls.

Host a Socratic Seminar on Affective Development

Using Socratic seminar, explore some of the questions that Carol Gilligan wrestled with such as:

- ◆ How do your relationships with others impact the decisions you make, particularly moral or ethical decisions?
- ◆ How does historical context impact our emotional development and decision-making process?
- ◆ How do care and compassion influence the choices we make? How does the absence of care and compassion influence our choices?
- ◆ Is it possible to develop a predictable algorithm or model for emotional development? Why or why not?

Process Comics

Drawing on our conversations around Drs. Simmons's and Gilligan's work, choose one or two of the terms and create a comic illustrating how it is a process (something you are always striving toward), not an outcome (something you have achieved).

- ◆ Racial justice
- ◆ SEL
- ◆ Healing
- ◆ Relationships

Lesson 2: One Child . . . Can Change the World

Malala Yousafzai (1997–) famously said, "One child, one teacher, one book, and one pen can change the world" (United Nations, 2013, 16:36). A Pakistani activist and advocate for girls' education, Yousafzai was targeted and shot in the face by the Taliban on her way home from school when she was 15 years old. Instead of silencing her as the Taliban intended, however, her injury had the opposite effect. After months of hospitalization and recovery, Yousafzai renewed her efforts to champion education for girls, which led her to co-found the Malala Fund, speak at the United Nations, and write the international bestsellers *I Am Malala: The Story of a Girl Who Stood up for Education and Was Shot by the Taliban* and *We Are Displaced: My Journey and Stories from Refugee Girls Around the World*. In 2014, Malala Yousafzai became the youngest person to win the Nobel Peace Prize.

Our values, beliefs, and experiences point us to specific issues we care about. Following are a few examples of young people we (Kathryn and Jill) know.[4]

◆ Beth opened up to her best friend Rachel about her struggles with depression. Rachel told Beth that she was there for her. A few months later, the two friends launched a t-shirt campaign to raise awareness for mental health.

◆ Roy was devastated when his cousin was killed by a drunk driver. As a project for his school honor society, he found a way to put these big, difficult feelings to use and partnered with a student organization to support a free rides program.

◆ Ana's teacher told her class about a nearby shelter that offers free housing to families while their children receive treatment for cancer. After Ana learned about the shelter's mission, she organized a school-wide drive to collect and deliver toys, clothes, and food to the shelter.

Each of these stories was sparked by interest, experience, and relationships. We are all influenced by the people around us.

When you care deeply about something, your voice and talents often speak more confidently to work toward change. Malala Yousafzai used her voice to expand educational opportunities first for girls in Pakistan and then from all over the world. She did not come from fortune, fame, or power. She was an ordinary person who made an extraordinary difference. Change is often sparked by ordinary moments, everyday experiences, and the relationships that make us human.

Think about all of the parts of your life that make you feel something in a strong way. Some of these issues might be very personal, like the way your friends treat one another. Others may be local, like the cleanliness of your nearest water supply. Still others might be global, like SDG 1 around poverty. Follow the steps below to identify an issue you care deeply about.

Step 1: Brainstorm and identify three defining experiences you have had.

1.
2.
3.

Step 2: What are the top two lessons these experiences taught you?

1.
2.

Step 3: What is one way these experiences and lessons might spark you to make a difference on an issue you care about?

Find a partner or small group and answer these questions:

◆ What issue did you identify? Whom does it impact and how?
◆ What experiences led you to learn about this issue? How and when has this issue mattered in your own life or community?
◆ What will you do to make a positive difference in this area that you care about?

Lesson 3: Audre Lorde—"The Uses of Anger"

Born in 1934 in New York City, **Audre Lorde** was the daughter of immigrant parents from the West Indies. As a child, when people asked how Audre Lorde was feeling, she would respond with a poem she had memorized. When the poems she memorized could no longer adequately express those feelings, she began writing her own poetry (Poetry Foundation, 2021).

Lorde served as a school librarian, poet, essayist, and activist. She identified herself as a "black, lesbian, mother, warrior, poet" (Poetry Foundation, 2021). Lorde used her creative genius to address social injustices related to racism, sexism, classism, and homophobia. In 1980, she released a personal account of her struggles with breast cancer, including her mastectomy. This work, *The Cancer Journals*, is still an acclaimed work on illness. The following year (1981), she and fellow feminist writers Cherríe Moraga and Barbara Smith founded Kitchen Table: Women of Color Press (Poetry Foundation, 2021). This press is credited as the first U.S. publisher dedicated to the writings of women of color.

"The Uses of Anger"—Audre Lorde

The essay you are studying today, "The Uses of Anger" is a speech Lorde wrote for her keynote address at the National Women's Studies Association Conference in 1981, the same year Kitchen Table was founded.

Anger is a complex, powerful, and universal emotion. Lorde says that "Anger is loaded with information and energy" (1981 Audre Lorde, "The Uses of Anger: Women Responding to Racism," 2012). We all feel anger, and it can be destructive to express that anger inappropriately. However, it can also be equally destructive not to express anger at all. Soraya Chemaly, who wrote a book about women's anger called *Rage Becomes Her*, says that "anger is the language of justice" (Norris, 2018, para 1). The key is to discover the best way to channel that anger, that information and energy and language of justice, into action.

 Essay Analysis Gallery Walk

Teaching Notes

Post the following quotes and questions from Lorde's speech around the room. Give scholars Post-It notes to write responses to the quotes and questions. In addition to sharing their own thoughts, they can also post responses to their peers. This activity can also work in the virtual classroom using Jamboard or other collaborative tools

Information and Energy

Anger is loaded with information and energy. If I participate, know-ingly or otherwise, in my sister's oppression and she calls me on it, to answer her anger with my own only blankets the substance of our exchange with reaction. It wastes energy. And yes, it is very difficult to stand still and to listen to another woman's voice delineate an agony I do not share, or one to which I myself have contributed.

(para 22)

◆ How is anger loaded with information and energy?
◆ Why is it important "to stand still and listen"?

Symphony of Anger

Women of Color in America have grown up within a symphony of anger at being silenced . . . And I say *symphony* rather than *cacopho-ny* because we have had to learn to orchestrate those furies so that they do not tear us apart. We have had to learn to move through them and use them for strength and force and insight within our daily lives.

(para 29)

◆ What are some examples of women of color being silenced?
◆ What is the difference between anger being a "symphony" and anger being a "cacophony"?

Stand Still and Listen

It is not the anger of other women that will destroy us but our refusal to stand still, to listen to its rhythms, to learn within it, to move beyond the manner of presentation to the substance, to tap that anger as an important source of em-powerment.

(para 31)

◆ How can refusing to listen to the rhythm of anger be destructive?
◆ How can anger be an important source of empowerment?

I Am Not Free

I am not free while any woman is unfree, even when her shackles are very different from my own. And I am not free as long as one person of Color remains chained. Nor is anyone of you.

(para 42)

- What are different ways that women and other marginalized communities are not free?
- Why is no one free unless everyone is free?

Think, Pair, Share

Spend some time with these reflective questions:

- How is anger a good thing?
- In our society, who has, and who does not have, permission to be angry?
- What can happen if anger is not expressed?
- Why is anger important in social justice work?
- How can anger fuel art and artistic movements?

Unit 4—Art as Resistance

Learning and teaching are inherently creative, visual, and expressive acts. From 2007 to 2010, I (Kathryn) taught at a public arts integration school in the Bay Area. I worked with incredible arts teachers, including Miranda Bergman, one of the muralists of the famous *MaestraPeace* mural (see Lesson 2). These experiences taught me that it is impossible to separate art from education. At this particular school, we created murals to teach and transform our communities. We recorded CDs, published a bilingual book of poems, and put on performances on peace and nonviolence. These were formative experiences in my teaching journey.

In 2014, I conducted a youth participatory action research project with a group of young women artists at a public high school in the Midwest. These scholars deepened my understanding of how the arts can be a transformative tool for inquiry, justice, and voice. Our project culminated in an art show on mental health exploring the social-emotional needs of young women on the precipice of high school graduation. These young artists were boldly creating art to make a statement. Said differently, their art was an act of resistance. In this unit, your scholars learn from artists engaged in resistance about who art is for, what counts as art, where art can (or should) be displayed, and how art can help us tell expansive and representative stories from a place of radical hope.

There are so many artists and activists engaged in this important and inspiring work that it felt impossible to choose a few to include herein. And yet, eventually, the deadline came on this unit, and decisions had to be made.[5] We (Kathryn and Jill) chose artists who represent a diversity of lived experiences and who offered or are offering ideas about the production of knowledge in feminism, art, and feminist art. We (Jill and Kathryn) are proud to include works that demand attention and works that have courageously reimagined space, craft, and story. To borrow from the definition of WGST shared in Chapter 1, these works are in themselves interdisciplinary studies of (1) the ways gender is constructed and how it affects our lived experiences and opportunities; (2) a commitment to work toward greater justice and equity; and (3) the intentional centering of stories, histories, and contributions of women and girls that are too often missing from curricula and media.

Teaching Notes: Close Reading of Images and Creating Art

When asked about her macro paintings of flowers, Georgia O'Keeffe, the American artist said, "Nobody sees a flower—really—it is so small it takes time—we haven't time—and to see takes time, like to have a friend takes time" (n.d.). Part of O'Keefe's work was to inspire people to pay attention, to see things differently, to notice, and to take the time to do so thoughtfully.

To read an image takes time. Just like story and literature, art images can be closely read for meaning, form, and structure. Throughout this unit, we will analyze several artists' work. On page 89-90 is a reproducible protocol for close reading of images. As O'Keeffe mentions, this kind of close reading takes time. To scaffold this literacy skill, you may find that it is helpful to work through these questions together as a whole class. As you continue reading images together, you might encourage scholars to use the full version, or you might choose to focus on one or two key rows for your analysis work.

During this unit, scholars will also create their own art. Each lesson includes an opportunity for artistic creativity after the artist or works being studied. Different scholars may have different comfort levels with drawing or creating art. It may help to have a conversation upfront about this where we acknowledge that we are all works in progress and that in this classroom space, we practice courage together. The artists included in this lesson use a wide range of media, including collage, drawing, painting, and performance art. We hope that scholars find joy and success in testing out some of these new methods. Your class norms can reinforce that this is a space for drafting, exploring, and testing out ideas. As scholars create, sketch, or plan their works, the expectation is not perfection. All learning is a process.

After you have completed the art lessons, scholars will return to their earlier works and select one to focus on and prepare for a class-organized public event. If possible, you may want to collaborate with an art teacher or community artists to support students with technical skills or questions as they finalize their favorite piece. A few well-taught strategies for drawing, shading, or texture can go a long way in supporting scholars' confidence in this creative endeavor.

Key Term: *Resistance*

1. The act of opposing a force
2. The refusal to give in
3. Being able to withstand strong forces

There are many ways to practice resistance and stand up to injustice. Resistance can include physical, emotional, verbal, and creative acts. The scholars, artists, changemakers, and writers in this book are resisting sexism, violence, gendered expectations, discrimination, and other social injustices. They are doing so in ways that are bold and brave, in ways that are big and small, and, with hope, each act of resistance moves us closer to a more honest story, a new connection, and ultimately a more humane version of our world.

Lesson 1: Feminist Art Movement

Term	Definition
Feminist Art Movement	An expansive multi-media arts movement that sought to (1) provide greater gender representation in art, (2) correct for and expose the erasure of women's stories and full identities, (3) and resist the reproduction of gender stereotypes in art (Rise Art, 2021).

The civil rights and social justice movements of the mid to late 1960s contributed to what is now called the *Feminist Art Movement*. Artists and activists during this period

> sought to rewrite a falsely male-dominated art history, change the contemporary world around them through their art, intervene in the established art world, and challenge the existing art canon. Feminist Art created opportunities and spaces that previously did not exist for women and minority artists.
>
> (The Art Story, n.d., para 1)

This lesson introduces scholars to some of the central beliefs and aims of the Feminist Art Movement(s) of the later half of the 20th century, which led to both the Identity Art and Activist Arts movements of the 1980s.

The lesson opens with works from two artists from this movement, Emma Amos, *Preparing for a Face Lift*, and Miriam Schapiro, *Costume for Mother Earth*.

Emma Amos—*Preparing for a Face Lift*

Emma Amos (1937–2020) was an African American artist whose mixed-media art included painting, weaving, printmaking, and textiles. Amos's work focused on themes of racism and sexism. She once said that "as a Black woman, just walking into a studio was a 'political act'" (*Emma Amos*, n.d.). One art piece by Amos included in a Brooklyn Museum exhibit called *We Wanted a Revolution: Black Radical Women, 1965–85* is called *Preparing for a Face Lift*. You can find this piece online, and a link is also included in the appendix.

First Read—Take a moment to take in the piece.
- ◆ What stands out to you or calls your attention?
- ◆ Does the piece invite you in and appeal to your sensibilities?

- ◆ Does the piece try to evoke a feeling, document an event, or present an idea?
- ◆ What story do you think the artist is telling?

The Brooklyn Museum described *Preparing for a Face Lift* this way: "Emma Amos's wry work on paper mimics several tropes of fashion magazines, transferring the advice column model of self-improvement to her experience as a Black woman trying to make it in the art world. Here she scrutinizes the physical toll of racism and sexism and the tyranny of cultural expectations for women's beauty" (#*Thosewhoinspireus: Emma Amos*, 2020).

Miriam Schapiro—*Costume for Mother Earth*

Miriam "Mimi" Schapiro (1923–2015) was a painter, sculptor, printmaker and a pioneer of feminist art. Born in Canada, the granddaughter of Russian immigrants, Schapiro lived most of her life in the United States. She coined the term *femmage* for her unique arts style, which challenged the ways "crafts," including quilting, collage, and textiles, were often regarded as "women's crafts" and not "fine art." Her femmages came out of the minimalist style of her time. While they preserved a strong appreciation for geometry, she shifted the style viewers expected by collaging it with doilies, weavings, bits of fabric, and purposeful bursts of feminist themes and content. In addition to femmage, Schapiro was one of the first artists to use computers in the design process. As a teacher, Schapiro encouraged art students to bring their full, complex identities to their work. In addition to her gendered lived experiences, Schapiro also often brought in aspects of Russian and Jewish identities.

Many images of Schapiro's diverse works are easily searchable online. As an introduction to her femmage style, explore *Costume for Mother Earth* as a class community. This piece was created in 1995 and measured 71 ½ x 51 ½ inches. As we continue learning to read images more closely, facilitate a conversation around context and connection in this piece.

Context and Connection—How is this piece in conversation or conflict with your own experiences in life or art?

- ◆ When was the piece created and for what purpose?
- ◆ What do you know about the artist?
- ◆ How does this background information influence your reading of the piece?

◆ How does this piece relate to other art you have analyzed?

◆ How does this piece connect to current events or literature you have studied?

◆ How does this piece connect with your own lived experiences? If you were creating a similar work, what choices would you make and why?

It's Your Turn—Respond Through Art

◆ **Option 1: Fashion Magazine Art**—In the spirit of *Preparing for a Face Lift*, create an art piece that uses the design of a fashion magazine cover to make a statement about racism, sexism, and cultural expectations of beauty. Amos used crayons to create her work, and scholars can choose to use crayons or colored pencils, pens, markers, paints, and words and pictures cut out of magazines.

◆ **Option 2: Create a Femmage**—In the spirit of *Costume for Mother Earth*, use collage materials that are important to you and that help tell the story of an issue or experience you care deeply about. Many of Schapiro's pieces worked within a geometric shape such as a half circle or square, and many played with scale. Have fun selecting everyday materials to tell a unique story that only you can tell.

Lesson 2: *MaestraPeace*—San Francisco Women's Mural

Term	Definition
Mural	A painting or work of art made directly on a wall or building.

Connecting to Prior Knowledge

◆ Do you know of any murals in your community? If so, where are they? What is their purpose or message?

◆ Do you know any artists who have worked on a mural?

◆ What else do you know about murals?

◆ What else would you like to learn about creating murals?

Painted on the Women's Building in San Francisco Mission District, the *MaestraPeace* **Mural** is one of San Francisco's largest and most famous murals. Maestra means teacher (feminine) in Spanish. The mural title means "Woman, Teacher of Peace." It was painted in 1994 by seven Bay Area muralists—Juana Alicia, Miranda Bergman, Edythe Boone, Susan Kelk Cervantes, Meera Desai, Yvonne Littleton, and Irene Perez—and restored in 2012. According to their website, the Women's Building is a "women-led community space that advocates self-determination, gender equality, and social justice" (The Women's Building, 2019, para 6) and the mural serves as a "visual testament to the courageous contributions of women through time and around the world" (The Women's Building, 2019, para 2). They welcome 25,000 clients and visitors a year.

Teaching Note

There are many images of the San Francisco Women's Building mural *MaestraPeace* available online. Project these for the class to view or allow scholars to do their own research and settle on an image that speaks to them. Using the close reading protocol (pp. 89-90), give scholars space to take a reflective beat and respond to the *MaestraPeace* mural.

Designing a Women's Mural

Like the *MaestraPeace* muralists, work as a team to design and plan your own women's mural. Following are some questions to guide your planning.

Central message: What central message(s) do you want to share with your mural?	◆ What will you title your mural? ◆ When people view your mural, what feelings and ideas do you hope to invoke? ◆ Where would be the ideal building or place for your specific mural?
Form: How will you use line, color, texture, and space to tell your story?	◆ Will you use bright, vivid colors or muted and understated tones? ◆ What textures will you include in your mural? ◆ How will you use light and space?
Inclusion: Whose voices and stories will you include in your mural?	◆ Will your mural include specific famous people? If so, who? ◆ Will your mural include everyday people engaged in everyday activities? If so, what will they be doing?
Story: How will your design choices enhance your messaging?	◆ What activities, scenes, and behaviors will be visible on your mural? ◆ Will you use any structures such as beginning-middle-end to lead viewers through a story? ◆ Will your mural include only images or text as well?

Name_____ Date_____

Close Reading for Images—A Viewing Protocol

Title_____ Artist_____

First Read

This step is similar to how you might skim a nonfiction work before diving in. Take a moment to take the piece in. What stands out to you or calls your attention? Do you feel drawn to this piece or uncertain about it?

Color and Light

How does the artist use color and light? Are the colors bright and vivid or muted and understated? Follow the light in the piece. What do you notice? Are the colors and use of light realistic or exaggerated? How do these choices contribute to the overall tone of the piece?

Texture and Line

How is texture and line used in this piece? Is this piece realistic? Abstract? Exaggerated? If so, how? What textures or lines catch your eye? Does the piece seem flat and two-dimensional or more curved and three-dimensional? How do these choices contribute to the overall tone of the piece?

Space and Movement

How do your eyes move along the piece? What design choices has the artist made to help tell their story? How are they using negative and positive space in this piece? How do the different elements in this piece work together?

Used with permission from Fishman-Weaver and Clingan, Teaching Women's and Gender Studies. Copyright © 2023, Taylor and Francis, Inc.

Close Reading for Images—A Viewing Protocol

Emotion and Message What message do you think the artist was trying to make with this piece? How does this image make you feel? What does this image make you think of? Are there spaces that surprise you or moments where the artist has clearly taken a risk?			
Context When was the piece created and for what purpose? What do you know about the artist? How does this background information influence your reading of the piece?			
Connection How does this piece connect to other art you have analyzed? How does this piece connect to current events or literature you have studied? Finally, how is this piece in conversation or conflict with your own lived experiences?			
Critical Thinking Response Just as with literature, your lived experiences and reading of this piece matter in how you interpret it. Review your notes in this table. Write a few summarizing sentences on the strategies the artist used to convey their message or create this piece and any key connections you made to this piece or the artist's overall message.			

Used with permission from Fishman-Weaver and Clingan, Teaching Women's and Gender Studies. Copyright © 2023, Taylor and Francis, Inc.

Lesson 3: Shamsia Hassani—Street Art as Resistance

> ### 💡 Thought Question: When Is Art a Form of Resistance?
>
> | Term | Definition |
> | --- | --- |
> | Street art | Art that is created on public spaces, including buildings, walls, and trains. |

"Art changes people's minds and people change the world," writes Shamsia Hassani (Shamsia Hassani—Official Website, 2021), who has gained acclaim and attention as Afghanistan's first woman street artist.

Street artists, also sometimes known as graffiti artists or public artists, are a diverse group, and many street artists come from identity backgrounds that experience discrimination, exclusion, silencing, and violence. According to an article on street art activism in the *Harvard Political Review*, "If you are a street artist, there's a higher chance of you being low-income, a person of color, female, or part of the LGBTQIA+ community" (Choi, 2020, para 6). In addition to challenging whom art is for, street art also challenges what spaces count as art spaces. Street art represents expansive thinking about the form and function of art. It is often a reclaiming of voice, as well as an act of resistance against silencing stories. Hassani's work offers a bold and powerful voice for Afghan women.

According to her website (Shamsia Hassani—Official Website, 2021), Hassani's art

> gives Afghan women a different face, a face with power, ambitions, and willingness to achieve goals. The woman character used in her artworks portrays a human being who is proud, loud, and can bring positive changes to people's lives. During the last decade of the post-war era in Afghanistan, Shamsia's works have brought in a huge wave of color and appreciation to all the women in the country.
>
> (para 2)

Connecting to Prior Knowledge
- What do you know about street art and what would you like to learn about street art?
- Do you know any street artists?
- Are street art and mural work the same or different? How so?

◆ How does street art contribute to our themes of resistance, representation, and radical hope?

Virtual Gallery Field Trip

Shamsia Hassani offers an extensive collection of her artwork for viewing on her website. Visit her exhibition collection linked at the end of this chapter. Choose an exhibit or two and spend some time exploring her art as class. As you do, use our close viewing protocol (pp. 89-90) and discuss one question per image.

Close Reading

Choose one of Hassani's works that resonates with you and spend time closely reading it with our close reading protocol (pp. 89-90).

Your Turn—Street Art in Chalk

> **Teaching Note**
>
> This activity asks scholars to create street art in chalk in their school yard. You will be the best judge of whether this activity requires any advanced approvals based on your school context. You will also be the best judge of whether there are additional guidelines you need to share regarding images or language used in the street art event. You might ask scholars to share sketches of their proposed street art images with you in advance of the event to workshop together.

Hassani's work shines an affirming spotlight on women in Afghanistan. The woman in her work is proud and visible and often shown through the lens of radical hope. Like Wanuri Kahiu's work, this is a work committed to telling more complete stories of Afghanistan.

◆ What stories do you want to tell?
◆ What message do you think others in your school community need to hear about justice, inclusion, gender rights, or belonging?

Plan a street art in chalk event to tell these stories in your school yard.

Lesson 4: Christine ("CK") Sun Kim, Sound Artist

 Thought Questions

- ◆ What is the sound of temperature rising?
- ◆ What is the sound of passing time?

Sound artist Christine Sun Kim explores these questions in her series "The Sound Of. . . ."[6]

Term	Definition
American Sign Language (ASL)	The sign language most used in the United States Deaf community. It is a language composed of hand motions, body movements, and facial expressions.

Christine ("CK") Sun Kim (1980–), the daughter of Korean immigrant parents, is an American sound artist based in Berlin. She uses drawing, performance, and video to explore how sound functions in society. Her unique and rich perspective to this theme is informed by her identity as a Deaf person. Much like other artists who have remarked that their art or identity is political, Kim says that belonging to the Deaf community is political. "I constantly questioned the ownership of sound," Kim says, "now I'm reclaiming sound as my property" (Artsy, n.d., para 1).

Deaf people continue to face discrimination, erasure, and injustice in both overt and covert ways. For example, Deaf people are often unemployed or underemployed, and Deaf women are six times more likely to be sexually assaulted than hearing women (The World, 2020). They also face a myriad of microaggressions, including being ignored, excluded, patronized, and bullied. Kim tackles these injustices headfirst in works such as "Deaf Rage" and "Trauma, LOL" using pie charts and graphs to diagram her lived experiences and illustrate the *obtuse, acute*, and *legit (right angle) rage* she experiences navigating an unjust and often inaccessible world.

The Enchanting Music of Sign Language

Listen to Christine Sun Kim's TED Talk on "The Enchanting Music of Sign Language" and then respond to the following questions.

- ◆ Why is "p" Kim's favorite musical annotation?
- ◆ What role does sound play in her life? What unique wisdom/perspective does she bring to understanding sound?
- ◆ Kim shares,

So I decided to reclaim ownership of sound and to put it into my art practice. And everything that I had been taught regarding sound, I decided to do away with and unlearn. I started creating a new body of work. And when I presented this to the art community, I was blown away with the amount of support and attention I received.

(4:56)

What is something you would like to unlearn or reclaim and why?

A Sensory Study
Choose one of your five senses: sight, hearing, taste, touch, or smell. For the next several days, pay attention to how this sense functions in your life.

Which sense are you focusing on? _____ |

Date	Observations and Lessons
	Pay attention to how you and others experience this sense. ◆ What do you notice that you missed before? ◆ What emotions do you connect to this sense? ◆ What are your takeaways from this study?

Let's create! By paying attention to the world and your experiences, you can identify areas to celebrate and areas in need of change. After spending several days or weeks observing this sense with new intentionality, create an art piece on your sensory study. Like Kim, you might create a chart, a graph, performance piece, or drawing. Connect your art to our WGST lessons about celebration and change.

Concept Synthesis Project: Emotion and Resistance

Name_____Date_____

The Work

During this unit, you have started drafting some of the following artworks:

- ◆ A woman's mural (after *MaestraPeace*)
- ◆ A femmage (after Miriam Schapiro)
- ◆ A deconstructed fashion magazine cover (after Emma Amos)
- ◆ Street art in chalk (after Shamsia Hassani)
- ◆ A sensory study (after Christine Sun Kim)

Choose one of these pieces to revisit and develop into your best work. Your piece should illustrate one or more of our course themes: *representation, resistance,* and *radical hope.* As you plan your piece, consider the presence of joy and/or anger in the message or story you are telling. All media, including mixed-media and performance, are welcome. You may work independently or in a collaborative group. If you are working in chalk or engaged in performance art, please also take images or video of your final piece.

Tip: Refer to the *Close Reading Protocol* for elements to consider in your own work.

Artist Statement

Each artist will submit an individual artist statement about their piece. Below is some guidance for your artist statement.

Title	What is the title of this work? What is the meaning of the title?
Thesis	What is the main message of your piece? What do you want viewers to learn or experience when they read your work?
Lived experiences	How does this piece connect to you and your peers' lived experiences? What does the viewer learn about you in reading this work? How is joy and/or anger present in this piece?
Course theme(s)	How does your piece illustrate or show a commitment to resistance, representation, or radical hope? Be specific.
Inspiration	Give a brief background on the artist(s) who inspired you. This may also be a good place to discuss the materials you chose to use in creating your art and why you chose those materials or media.

Used with permission from Fishman-Weaver and Clingan, Teaching Women's and Gender Studies. Copyright © 2023, Taylor and Francis, Inc.

Extension Exercises for Concept 2

"Uses for Anger" Audre Lorde With Christine Sun Kim

When studying Audre Lorde's speech "Uses for Anger," you learned about how important anger can be in movements for justice. Artist Christine Sun Kim has found a unique way to express her anger. Explore Kim's pie charts from her *Deaf Rage* series. Pay attention to how Kim uses both humor and seriousness to make her points. What is an issue that makes you angry? Create a pie chart in the style of CK Kim to bring about awareness of the issue.

Self-Portraits and Portraits—The Women Who Inspire Us

Frida Kahlo (1907–1954) was a Mexican painter. Her distinct style, intimate self-portraits, use of bold color, and use of raw storytelling are celebrated around the world. Kahlo told deeply personal and embodied stories in her work. She also used heavy symbolism, including dark images.

◆ Read more about Kahlo's life and the ways she processed her lived experiences through her work. Engage in a close read of *Roots, 1943*, which showcases many of Kahlo's signature choices.

Many feminist artists (as well as Indigenous rights activists and LGBTQ+ rights activists) have admired Kahlo's work. One such artist is **Miriam Schapiro**, whom we learned about in this lesson.

◆ Engage in a close read of *Conservatory (Portrait of Frida Kahlo)* painted by Miriam Shapiro in the 1980s. Schapiro created this piece using her own signature femmage style, which we also learned about.

◆ After reading the images independently, consider how they are in conversation with each other. What similarities and differences do you notice? How do you think Kahlo would react to Schapiro's self-portrait? Defend your response. If you were to create a portrait of an artist you admire, who would you choose and why?

Yolanda López

Yolanda López (1942–2021) was a Chicana artist and activist. Her career in California spanned five decades. López often used her own image or that of her mother, grandmother, and other women in her family to bring about visibility of women, especially working class women, across life's stages (Museum of Contemporary Art San Diego, 2021). Like several of the artists included in this chapter, López often used scale in her work, painting and sketching her portraits larger than life.

◆ The Museum of Contemporary Art San Diego has put together a video and web page showcasing three iconic López images. This webpage is linked in our chapter appendix. View the three-minute video and then engage in a close reading of one of her images.
◆ Engage in a close read of *Grandmother,* from the series *Tres Mujeres/ Three Generations*, which stands 8 feet by 4 feet.

YOU. Create your own portrait (or self-portrait) of a woman who inspires you. How will you use the art elements we have studied in this chapter, including scale? How will you use symbolism?

Helpful Links
◆ "Wanuri Kahiu, Fun, Fierce, and Frivolous" TED Talk: www.ted. com/talks/wanuri_kahiu_fun_fierce_and_fantastical_african_art/ transcript?language=en#t-229123
◆ Mikela Henry-Lowe portrait work: www.mikelahenrylowe.com/#/
◆ "How Students of Color Confront Imposter Syndrome" TED Talk by Dena Simmons: www.youtube.com/watch?v=8sQ2p89P0Us (Great talk for educators)
◆ "The Uses of Anger" Speech by Audre Lorde: www.blackpast.org/ african-american-history/speeches-african-american-history/ 1981-audre-lorde-uses-anger-women-responding-racism/
◆ The SF Women's Mural: https://womensbuilding.org/the-mural/
◆ *Preparing for a Face Lift* by Emma Amos: https://journal.alabamach-anin.com/2020/07/thosewhoinspireus-emma-amos/
◆ On Miriam Schapiro, Femmage Morning Edition: www.wnyc.org/ story/review-miriam-schapiro-soon/
◆ Emma Amos—Georgia Musuem of Art: https://georgiamuseum. org/exhibit/emma-amos-color-odyssey/
◆ Shamsia Hassani's website: www.shamsiahassani.net/
◆ Shamsia Hassani's Exhibitions: www.shamsiahassani.net/exhibitions
◆ Christine Sun Kim's "The Enchanting Music of ASL": www.ted. com/talks/christine_sun_kim_the_enchanting_music_of_sign_ language?language=en
◆ Christine Sun Kim's *The World is Sound*, "Sound of . . ." series: www. youtube.com/watch?v=3vU4TCKxZlc
◆ Explore more of Frida Kahlo's works at www.fridakahlo.org

◆ *Note: Some of the images in this collection include graphic scenes. Teachers may want to preview images first and make choices about how best to process or explore them with their middle school communities.*
◆ Museum of Contemporary Art San Diego, "Portrait of the Artist" Yolanda Lopez: www.mcasd.org/exhibitions/yolanda-l%C3%B-3pez-portrait-artist

Notes

[1] Translated from Portuguese: *My voice I use to speak about what is silent.*
[2] This is a reference to Chimamanda Adichie, a Nigerian activist we also study in these lessons.
[3] You can find a link to these in the section appendix.
[4] We (Kathryn and Jill) have changed names and identifying details.
[5] In addition to the artists included in these lessons, you can also find additional artists and works in the extension resources. We also encourage you to celebrate local artists in your own communities.
[6] You can find a link to this series in the chapter appendix.

3

Diversity, Inclusion, and Representation

Concept Foreword by Lisa DeCastro, Advisory Editor

Lisa DeCastro *(she/her) currently serves as the elementary coordinator at Mizzou Academy. She has had the privilege of learning and laughing with kindergarten and first grade students and believes in the value of all student voices, especially those of our youngest learners. Lisa lives in California with her husband, two sons, and beloved four-legged Weimaraner, Gunther. As the only woman in her family, one of her most important jobs is raising kind and compassionate sons. Her perfect day begins with a brisk morning walk, watering her plants, and sitting in her backyard, coffee in hand, and reading the newspaper.*

One of my earliest memories from school is reading to my classmates in the library nook of Miss O'Brien's first grade classroom. The book I chose was *Lisa and Lynn* by Dick Bruna. I have no recollection of what the simple story was about other than this was my favorite book because *my* name was on the front cover. It didn't matter that the character, Lisa, with blonde pigtails and fair skin, looked nothing like me. I was a girl, had pigtails, but they were black—we shared the same name, and that was enough for me. With pride, I sat in the rocking chair and read *Lisa and Lynn* to my classmates sitting on the rug in front of me.

When I reflect on this memory, so many questions percolate in my mind. I yearn to ask my six-year-old self: *Do you remember any books that featured girls*

DOI: 10.4324/9781003289500-4

that looked like you or represented your Filipino-American family? Did I notice that all of the books and stories I read as a child, and even into my teens, had no characters that looked like me, my brother, or my family? To make my family even more unique, my family was intergenerational—my grandmother lived with us, and my mother worked full-time which was remarkably different from any family of my friends or in the neighborhood. Where were the books that told a story similar to mine?

In this closing section of *Teaching Women's and Gender Studies*, Kathryn and Jill inspire teachers and students to walk boldly and bravely on a journey to advance diversity, inclusion, and representation in their school communities. Today there are an increasing number of children's books that depict more diverse characters and are also written by more authors of color. As an adult, when I discovered the children's book, *Cora Cooks Pancit* by Dora K. Lazo Gilmore, my heart swelled with both pride and the feeling of "it's about time" for a book with characters who represent my childhood self and family. As educators, it is imperative that our students see themselves in the curriculum, books, and resources that we carefully choose to bring into our classrooms. Even in the years that have passed since being in the classroom, I have noticed there are a number of picture books that celebrate children and families with multicultural and diverse perspectives. Imagine schools with classroom libraries full of books that represent the tapestry of our multidimensional students. How would their identities be shaped when validated and represented? How would the self-confidence of neurodivergent students grow and blossom? How does that impact students' beliefs and actions toward inclusion? What message does it send?

Jill and Kathryn call upon us to continue affirming our students and to expand the affirmations to celebrations of gender and (dis)abilities. We know as adults and life-long learners that students build their confidence within themselves and others, take risks, and stand up for their beliefs when they are in a safe place and surrounded by caring and compassionate people. My own evolution as a teacher began by switching, "Good morning, boys and girls," to "Good morning, friends." More recently, I have been adding my pronouns to my name wherever I can, and using the terms such as "Latinx" to promote gender inclusion. These intentional choices that we make with our words may seem small but can yield many positives for humanity and compassion.

Our schools can be places of change, revolution, and inclusion when we embrace the growth that may stem from discomfort. Classroom discussions about representation and equity for LGBTQIA+ and disability communities can be unpredictable. Sharing feelings about gender identities and sexuality can be uncomfortable and may bring out the giggles from middle school students who are new to discussion of such topics. As teachers, we can model and show our students how to risk feelings of vulnerability and truths that may not have surfaced for us before, and we may not have the answers to where to put all these emotions. *Teaching Women's and Gender Studies* gives educators the place to start. This important work is rooted in justice, equity, and inclusion and cannot be done alone. Seek out and form partnerships to collaborate with other teachers at your school.

A few years ago, I had the opportunity to attend teacher leadership training where one session focused on a basic principle of improv comedy, "yes, and." The "yes" accepts the truth. The "and" determines the response and the desire to move forward. Imagine the power of "yes, and" when used to affirm differences and (dis)abilities as strengths, overcome challenges, and foster inclusion. I can hear Arianna in second grade saying, "Yes I have ADHD, and I keep trying to draw this monarch butterfly," or William, a high school sophomore saying, "Yes, I have dyslexia, and I will reread this chapter after school with my teacher." Throughout this section, Jill and Kathryn set the stage for teachers and students to embrace "yes, and" while embarking on a journey to discover and celebrate the power that comes from within each other and their communities. In the coming readings, discussions, and activities, students will share and reflect upon experiences and issues that matter to them, explore historic firsts of women in government, and learn from the wisdom and stories of ancestors. With tenacity in our hearts and standing on the shoulders of each other, we must keep looking for the light shining in the rainbows of radical hope. As Arundhati Roy (2004), the writer and activist, reminded us, "Another world is not only possible, she is on her way. On a quiet day, I can hear her breathing" (p. 86).

Teaching Concept Overview—Diversity, Inclusion, and Representation

Purpose: These closing units deepen our earlier lessons on feminisms, intersectionality, and justice work. They celebrate the ripple effect of both history-changing and everyday acts of advocacy. Drawing on representative and diverse examples of activists who have advanced racial justice, LGBTQIA+ inclusion, and disability rights work, these two units celebrate the power that comes from within communities. Like the lessons that precede them, these units teach scholars that their lived experiences are knowledge-rich and that their voices and leadership can make a positive difference right now. To solidify this message, Unit 6 concludes with scholars authoring an original policy proposal on a local justice issue.

✔ **Objectives**

By the end of these units, scholars will be able to:

◆ Define *artivism* and consider how art can be used to advance justice.
◆ Brainstorm strategies to make their school communities more gender affirming.
◆ Analyze biographies of activists who are expanding representation and equity for the LGBTQIA+ and disability communities.
◆ Connect the work of their ancestors and elders in the activist movements to current justice work.
◆ Author a policy proposal.

? Essential Questions for Scholars

◆ How will I advance justice and inclusion?
◆ What would it look like to live in a world that affirmed the full humanity of every person on the planet?
◆ Is it possible to right equity wrongs?
◆ What are my most important WGST takeaways?

⏸ Reflective Questions for Educators

◆ Can my scholars see themselves in my curriculum?
◆ How can I draw on ancestral and community knowledge in my curriculum?
◆ How will I support student leadership in my classes?

Activate Prior Knowledge—Day of Silence	
Unit 5—Our Vibrant World: Representation	**Unit 6—From Our Ancestors: Change Movements for A More Just World**
Lesson 1—Artivism: Activist Art for a More Just and More Vibrant World Lesson 2—Vibrance, Belonging, and Trans Representation Lesson 3—Disability Rights: Scholarship to Center and Celebrate Disability Lesson 4—The Ripple Effect of Being First: Representation in Government	Lesson 1—Is it Possible to Right Equity Wrongs? Lesson 2—Lessons from Our Grandmothers' Change Movements Lesson 3—Policy Proposal: A Catalyst for Justice
Synthesis Project—Toward Justice and Joy	

Teaching Notes

This concept includes the stories of many people who have fought for diversity, inclusion, and representation. Some of these people are nationally or internationally known. Others are not. While the *famous* stories are certainly inspiring and powerful, it is important to remember that the stories of our own neighbors, community members, and peers can be just as inspiring and powerful. In fact, these community-based narratives are the stories that often bring activism, advocacy, and history out of a textbook and into one's own community, classroom, and home.

While teaching this unit, we (Kathryn and Jill) encourage you to invite local activists, changemakers, artists, and leaders to come speak to your class. Who are the people working to advance racial and gender justice in your towns or cities? Who is addressing food insecurity, homelessness, and access to health care in your community? Who is speaking up on issues related to these lessons in your newspaper, at city council meetings, or on the local school board? Who is threading care in quieter ways, sending children home with snacks on the weekend, visiting the elderly, including peers in extracurriculars, standing up to bullies, and creating safe spaces in your communities? These (extra)ordinary stories invite us to each do what we can everyday to advance the progress of representation, resistance, and radical hope in own communities.

Concept Dedications

Kathryn's Dedication—When this book is published, my youngest, Lilah, will be a new middle school student. As a fierce changemaker and justice-seeker, she holds my section dedication.

Like a lot of the young people I work and learn with, Lilah has many passions and endless faith that a better world is possible. Several years ago, she launched two annual food drives. Through her efforts, each year, we are able to donate over 1,000 lb of food to our mid-Missouri food bank. Lilah serves monthly at our local soup kitchen, where she has developed meaningful relationships with community members who are navigating housing insecurity. In fact, on the nights that Lilah serves, she runs the whole food line and does so with tremendous compassion, often teaching new volunteers how to serve with humanity. Lilah is also an artist and has partnered with her dad to sell alcohol ink paintings as a fundraiser for CASA (court-appointed special advocates for youth in foster care).

She is well-read on racial justice issues, often teaching our whole family new things at the dinner table. She loves to learn and views learning as a necessary tool for change. Lilah offered to serve as a research assistant for this book. She sent Jill and me articles and links on trans representation and women's history and gave us notes on several of the graphic organizers.

At the time, she was ten years old.

This closing section celebrates the power of youth leadership and advocacy. The young people we know aren't waiting until they "grow up" to make a difference. Like the scholars in your classes, they are showing up for their communities and teaching us all that we belong to each other.

Jill's Dedication—I dedicate this chapter to a young man who asked me to call him Terrance. When I curled up on his couch one evening to chat with him, one of the very first things he said to me was, "Being trans is not the highest thing on my list of what makes me interesting." I agree. Terrance is super smart, funny, passionate, and kind. When I first met him, I was drawn to his huge smile, his big laugh, and his witty and wise take on things from the temporal to the philosophical.

While being trans is not the most interesting thing about Terrance, he does have an interesting story to tell. He is one of those young people who, tragically, ticks up the statistics by organizations like the Trevor Project. He ran away from home, was kicked out of his home, struggled with depression, and tried to commit suicide. With the exception of his Nana, who has been accepting of him since the day he told her he was trans, most of his family were—and still are—not accepting of his gender identity. He said,

> I had to unlearn a lot of biases I was taught as a child. You have to re-teach yourself, "No, I don't deserve to be treated like that. I'm a human person. And how many people are like me in the world?" The biggest thing I have tried to fight for is to be regular. I just want to be seen and respected for how I feel and who I am.

While Terrance did not feel safe at home, he did feel safe at school. He had two teachers who were especially supportive of him. He is still friends with his seventh grade English teacher, Mrs. K, who always checked to see if anyone was picking on him and made sure he was okay. Before she retired from teaching, she started a gay-straight alliance club at her middle school and invited him to come speak to the LGBTQ young people there. A guidance counselor in high school, Ms. M, also meant a great deal to him. She made sure his name was correct on the class rosters, helped him get on the boys' wrestling team, and when he was homeless found him a shelter to go to.

As Terrance noted, "Knowing you are trans and starting the transition is the easy part. I think it's asserting yourself as someone new in the world that's the hard part." He found that it was the teachers and educators in his life who "helped me feel safe. They were amazing supporters to me my entire youth." As I dedicate this chapter to Terrance, I also think of you, the educators who can be the "Mrs. K" and "Ms. M" in your scholars' lives, educators who advocate for and support your LGBTQIA+ scholars, educators who provide a safe space for these young people as they discover who they are.

Concept Introduction by Kathryn and Jill

How do you respond to the sexist joke, the school bully, the erasure in curricula, the friend who is hurting? The lessons in these units invite principled action toward these and other big questions. They explore broad policy changes alongside the everyday decisions (extra)ordinary people make to set their communities on a new path. When Claudette Colvin, a teenage girl who just learned about Sojourner Truth and Harriet Tubman in school, says, "No, I will not give up my seat just to make a White person more comfortable"; when Opal Lee, a grandmother in her 80s, laces up her sneakers to go on a multi-state mission to celebrate a more complete history; when scholars in Brazil turn a beauty pageant into a teach-in on racial justice; when a middle school student starts a campaign for gender inclusion in sports; something important shifts.

Every act of justice, equity, and inclusion creates ripples for continued justice, equity, and inclusion. Intentional and often incremental changes transform our communities, institutions, and government. By drawing on the inspiration of our ancestors, these lessons encourage scholars to be purposeful descendants, to create a world that is more just and more inclusive than the one they were born into. In these closing units, we (Kathryn and Jill) affirm that there is power within—power within each young person in your classrooms, power within your communities, your art, your creative process, and within the vibrant range of the human experience. We can't wait to see all the ways scholars will seek opportunities to transform their peer groups, classrooms, schools, and broader communities.

Educator Letter for Concept 3—*Take a Moment*

Dear Valued Educator,

By now, we are good friends. Come as you are. Wear your favorite old sweatshirt. Show up with uncombed hair and a half-drunk cup of coffee. As you embark on these last two units, we (Kathryn and Jill) want to shine a light on strategies that restore, celebrate, and leverage community resources. We also want to congratulate you on this important work, warm up our own cups of coffee to sip along with you, and hear the story of where that favorite sweatshirt came from and why you're not ready to let it go.

Your Work Matters

In several of the lessons in these units, you will support scholars in cultivating practices and changing policies to make your schools and communities more inclusive and affirming. This work can have a direct and immediate impact. In addition to these effects, which you may be able to see directly during the teaching of these units, there are positive ripples to this work that you may never fully know. Please remember that your work matters. Teaching and advocacy are life-changing endeavors. Thank you for all you do.

Care Strategies for Educators

- ◆ **Celebrate the good.** As part of cultivating a caring and reflective practice, take time to celebrate the successes from these lessons. It is easy to focus (or even ruminate) on the things that didn't go (or aren't going) the way you wanted. Part of a reflective practice is problem solving around these challenges. However, as important or maybe even more so, is taking a strengths-based perspective with your own teaching by pausing to consider what is going well and how you can build on that. Below are some questions to consider.
  - How have you seen your scholars grow as leaders, writers, artists, advocates, and critical thinkers?
  - How have you grown as a leader, writer, artist, advocate, and critical thinker?
  - In what ways is your curriculum and teaching practice stronger for having taught these units on Women's and Gender Studies?
  - What positive changes have you noticed in your class community?
  - What were your favorite activities from these lessons, and why do they stand out to you?
- ◆ **Connect your community.** Throughout this text, we (Kathryn and Jill) have encouraged you to lean on your community as a source of support. Reminding you that no one teaches, learns, or lives in a vacuum, we've encouraged you to pool the collective energies and talents of those around you.
  - What are other ways you can connect your communities to your work in the classroom?
  - Do you have an artist friend who could give a guest lesson on art projects?

- Do you have a friend in the business sector who could donate materials or space for events?
- Who are your friends' friends, and what connections do they have that might support your work? Consider nonprofits, politicians, and local leaders.
- Would your local paper be willing to cover a learning event in your classroom?
- Do you have an NPR member station that would invite young people to talk about their work?
- Is there a health clinic or gym in town that would be willing to guest teach on wellness and health disparities?

◆ The list goes on and on. These examples are real strategies that I (Kathryn) have used in my own classroom to gain access to materials and experts and to shine a light on the important work my scholars are doing. Lean on your connections to leverage possibilities, to celebrate your class community, and to show your scholars that your classroom extends far beyond four physical walls.

◆ **Take a moment to rest.** From action projects to advocacy work to intentionally expanding your curricula to make it more complete (and celebratory), you and your scholars have covered a lot of ground in these lessons. Across all the brave conversations, guest visits, and community work, you have committed to courageous learning.

As we come to these closing units, we (Jill and Kathryn) want to encourage you to mark this accomplishment and then take a beat to rest. Close the book. Close the lesson plans and the computer. Take a weekend to garden, to sleep, to cook, to hike, to do tasks that are rejuvenating and restorative. Taking care of yourself by resting and recharging not only gives you strength to continue engaging in this difficult and important work; it also models for your students that they, too, are full and beautiful humans who are more than the lessons they learn, the homework they submit, and the scores they earn in school. Rest, like joy, is a form of strength and resistance. Embrace it.

With admiration,

Kathryn and Jill

Activate Prior Knowledge

 Thought Questions

◆ When is a time you felt truly heard? What did that feel like? Who were you with, and what was happening?

◆ When is a time you wanted to share a truth, an answer, an opinion, or a story and couldn't do so? What did that feel like? Who were you with and what was happening?

◆ Compare these two situations. What can they teach us about power? Whose stories and whose voices do you think get heard the most, and whose are silenced or missing?

The consequences of silencing are deep and damaging. Silencing can look like erasure and marginalization. It can feel like being invalidated, forgotten, and unsafe. Silencing is a form of oppression. Like other acts of oppressions, activists can resist or speak back to silencing. Boycotts, protests, demonstrations, marches, and telling more complete and representative stories are all examples of ways activists have resisted silencing and oppression. In this activity, you will learn more about the National Day of Silence, which has been used to draw attention to the ways silencing impacts the LGBTQIA+ community.

About the National Day of Silence

GLSEN (the Gay, Lesbian, and Straight Education Network) organizes a National Day of Silence, which is a youth movement whose goal is to bring awareness to the ways LGBTQIA+ individuals are silenced in school. In some ways, this silencing is an act of omission, as LGBTQIA+ scholars are underrepresented in curriculum. In other ways, this silencing is an act of harassment, discrimination, and violence. In the United States, the National Day of Silence is observed in April. Students participate by taking a vow of silence for the day. While GLSEN's National Day of Silence is geared specifically towards LGBTQIA+ youth, silencing, inclusion, and equity are concepts that span Women's and Gender Studies and social justice issues.

Hold a Classwide Day of Silence

Implement a Day of Silence in your classroom.[1] Your *day* of silence may be a full day, a class period, or even just ten minutes. Even a few minutes of silence can have a powerful effect as scholars reflect on the ramifications of silenced voices. Your class may choose to focus on the silencing of LGBTQIA+ voices in schools, the experiences they reflected on through the questions provided earlier, or another justice issue affected by silencing and oppression.

During the period of silence, provide scholars with art supplies like paper, colored pens or pencils, markers, paints, crayons, or clay. Depending on the direction you take with this activity, you might offer the following reflection questions for scholars to consider.

- ◆ How have marginalized voices been silenced historically?
- ◆ In what ways are marginalized voices still silenced?
- ◆ What is the relationship between justice and silencing?
- ◆ What would a world look like in which voices were not silenced?

Break the Silence

While silence is a powerful tool of self-reflection, breaking that silence is also a powerful moment. Ask scholars to pause their art reflections for a moment right before ending this reflection time. Then, break the silence! Ask scholars to share their reflections about silencing and voice. Some scholars may want to share their answers to the reflection questions. Some scholars may want to share the meaning behind their reflective artwork.

To close the activity, ask scholars to respond to this sentence stem offered by GLSN:

I am breaking the silence because_____.

Unit 5—Our Vibrant World: Representation

While working on this unit, my (Kathryn's) childhood best friend texted me the joyous news of her daughter's arrival. Along with the sweetest picture, she sent a lengthy description of her daughter's name. The new babe's first name means "light" in Pakistani. My friend said we all needed more light, and I felt that deep in my soul. This unit, like all the units in the book, addresses weighty topics. In this unit, scholars explore ableism, transphobia, racism, and gender disparities in leadership. However, as we (Kathryn and Jill) wrote these lessons, we did so with a commitment to keep looking for the light. In highlighting activists, barrier breakers, and changemakers, the following lessons bring readers to Brazil, Cuba, the United States, the Philippines, Canada, Thailand, and India.

The opening lesson introduces scholars to *artvisim* and asks young people how they can use their creative talents to advance justice. From hip hop to dance to spoken word poetry, scholars get to practice the ways Amanda Gorman calls "using your voice is a political choice." The second lesson explores trans representation, everyday advocacy, and celebrates activists who are, as Tanwarin Sukkhapisit puts it, "writing a new political history." In Lesson 3, scholars engage with the intersection of disability rights and feminisms. Here they learn about the neurodiversity movement and perspectives that take an assets-based approach to disability, showing how neurodiversity is both necessary and valuable to the human experience. The final lesson in this unit addresses gender disparities in leadership and presents a partial timeline of historic firsts in the U.S. federal government. Scholars then research a key figure who helped shift representation in government.

We (Kathryn and Jill) hope these lessons plant seeds of promise. While some days are full of shadows and heartbreak, we have tried to write lessons that keep chasing the light. When I (Kathryn) get disheartened, I find nothing is more centering or promising than talking with young people. In this past week alone, I've heard from a high school student who created an inclusion initiative in partnership with the Special Olympics, a teenager who is launching a tutoring program for low-income youth in Brazil, and a student leader who organized a food drive in India. Each of these young people identified an issue in their local communities and then developed and implemented a plan to affirm the rights and dignity of their community members. As you move from this unit to the final unit, we (Kathryn and Jill) can't wait to hear all the ways your scholars will further this critical work.

Key Term: *Representation*

Representation is both inclusion and advocacy. Throughout these lessons, you have seen the ways oppression and marginalization limit who is included, whose stories are told and celebrated, and who has access to power and privilege. These lessons invite you to chase the light, to tell and listen to more complete and complicated stories, and to rewrite policy and practice as you work toward a more inclusive and vibrant world.

As you engage in work around representation, we (Kathryn and Jill) encourage you to use these five guiding questions:

- ◆ Whom do you speak for?
- ◆ What issues do you speak on?
- ◆ Who is included? Who is missing?
- ◆ Whose stories are centered and celebrated?
- ◆ Whose voices/perspectives do you still need to hear?

Lesson 1: Artivism—Activist Art for a More Just and More Vibrant World

Teaching Notes

This lesson includes many layers and activities and may take a few class periods to complete. Through the lesson, scholars will learn more about artivism (art + activism) and explore how beauty and power have been defined and redefined through creative social justice movements.

The lesson opens with a collage activity on beauty and power. If possible, ask scholars to bring magazines and newspapers to cut up, or you can provide these along with scissors and glue. This activity offers important opportunities to explore and revisit key course concepts including gender, social construction, marginalization, centering, and stereotypes. Encourage critical thinking in the discussion. Who is defining beauty and power, and what are the consequences of these definitions?

This leads right into some learning on Eurocentrism (lesson term) and the next activity on the Black is Beautiful Movement in the 1960s in the United States. Throughout this book, scholars have explored positive ripples. We continue this work in our approach to Black is Beautiful by next looking at a recent event in Brazil and to the global hashtag #BlackGirlMagic. In addition to the two videos referenced directly in the lesson, you can also find additional resources on hair love and natural hair in the section appendix.

This is a multimedia lesson. In addition to creating collages, scholars will also watch videos and explore readings together. As with all videos, please preview these ahead of time for your class context and to plan for any concepts that need additional scaffolding.

To help organize scholars' thinking throughout this big lesson, there is a PCR (prior knowledge-connections-research) graphic organizer available as a reproducible for this lesson.

Venn Diagram, (Re)Defining Beauty and Power—Create a Venn diagram with *Beauty* in one circle and *Power* in the other.

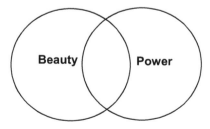

Using images and words from magazines and other available materials, create a collage that illustrates what these two terms mean to you separately and where they overlap. There are as many right answers to this task as there are people in our class.

 ## Take a Reflective Beat

Following some creative time, discuss these questions:

- What do you notice about the words and images you put in the beauty circle?
- What do you notice about the words and images you put in the power circle?
- Where do you see the intersection of the two?
- Who defines beauty?
- Who defines power?
- How is redefining power or beauty related to our studies in WGST?

Thought Questions

- Have you heard the phrases "Black is Beautiful" or "Black Girl Magic"?[2]
- How do these phrases relate to our activity on beauty and power?

This conversation isn't just about what counts as beautiful; it's about who counts to be celebrated, affirmed, and centered. Review the vocabulary terms below.

Term	Definition
Eurocentrism	Excluding or omitting the multiple global perspectives, experiences, cultures, and histories that make our world and casting European culture and history as the norm.
Political	Although often related to government work, in the context of our studies, *political* refers to the way an idea or an ideal translates to direct action.
Artivism	A combination of art and activism, whereby artists address injustice, inequities, and other social challenges through creative expression. Artivists aim to increase awareness of social issues and reimagine and reclaim new possibilities through their work. Artivists may use a variety of media, including slam poetry, music, dance, mural, performance art, large-scale installations, and graphic design.

Throughout this book, you have explored the creative ways activists are expanding access, telling more complete stories, redefining terms and systems, and working toward greater justice. Later in this lesson, you will study Amanda Gorman's 2018 TED Talk, "Using Your Voice is a Political Choice." Gorman's TED Talk is a poetic discourse on the connection between art and politics. As she notes, "All art is political. The decision to create, the artistic choice to have a voice, the choice to be heard is the most political act of all." In this lesson, you will meet activists and *artivists* who are using their creative powers for social good. Artivism has the potential to challenge racism, sexism, discrimination, and injustice; to raise awareness about inequities and injustice; and to help viewers imagine and work intentionally toward a more just reality.

Artists from all over the world are exploring the combination of creativity and activism to challenge inequities and create a new narrative. In Brazil, for example, artivists from Rio de Janeiro's poorest communities, the favelas, are helping to rewrite a new narrative about race, class, and gender. Carmen Martinez and Kerry Carrington (2021) studied art movements from the favelas and said that these works create a "paradigm of potential . . . and give visibility to another periphery which affirms itself through its agency, inventiveness, and nonviolent pathways." In particular, they cite passinho dancers[3] and slam poets as creators who are actively challenging patriarchy, racism, and heteronormativity through their art. In this lesson, you will meet artivists from the United States, Cuba, and Brazil who are using their creative talents to co-create and reimagine a more inclusive and beautiful world.[4]

Read the two short profiles below and respond to the questions that follow.

Reading I: Las Krudas (Cuba)

In 1996, Odaymara Cueta, Olivia "Oli" Prendes, and Oadlys Cuesta founded the first vegan and queer activist arts group in Havana, Cuba, called Cubensi. Their art expanded who hip hop was for and what hip hop could do. Their music centered "the social and economic reality of being Black and female in Cuba" (Armstead, 2007, p. 109), and their work has continued to expand to include trans and queer rights and continued gender justice work. In addition to performing, the group has strong roots in teaching and has brought music and theater to children in Cuba.

(▶) *View the Las Krudas music video* La Gorda, *which is linked in the section appendix. How does this connect to our conversations about beauty, gender, power, and representation?*

In 2006, Odaymara Cuesta and Oli Prendes immigrated to Texas in the United States and rebranded as Las Krudas. The duo self-identifies on their Krudas Cubensi website as "fat, feminist, queer, trans non-binary, black & brown vegan immigrants [who] are aware that most of these intersections are underrated in the music industry" (Krudas Cubensi, n.d.). Their lyrics address the intersectionalities of gender, race, class, power, and sexual orientation and challenge systems of discrimination and exploitation. Using music as an act of resistance against oppression, they celebrate and affirm a vibrant range of identities. The duo continues to perform and hold workshops across North and South American and the Caribbean (Archwy, 2021). The Kennedy Center (n.d.), one of the most acclaimed performing centers in the United States, writes that Las Krudas represents, "womyn, immigrants, queer and people of color action as a central part of world change."

Reading II: Miss Black Power Brazil (Brazil)

"A tapestry of European, African and Indigenous backgrounds that has defied the more rigid racial categories used elsewhere" (para 4) is how McCoy and Traiano described Brazil in their 2020 *Washington Post* article on race. Brazil is home to more people of African descent than any other country outside of Africa (McCoy and Traiano, 2020, para 4). Although race is a somewhat fluid construct in Brazil, racism and slavery continue to have a lasting impact on social reality in the country. Afro-Brazilians continue to carry the intergenerational trauma of slavery. In 1888, Brazil was the last country in the Western Hemisphere to abolish slavery (TBR Newsroom, 2019). Still today, economic, health, and employment dispar-ities continue to hurt Afro-Brazilians (Mitchell-Walthour, 2020). Police killings of Black people in Brazil are staggering with 5,800 Black people killed by the police in Brazil in 2019 (McCoy and Traiano, 2020).

And yet . . . and still . . . Afro-Brazilians are speaking out and step-ping boldly into the spotlight. As they do, they are helping their country and the world imagine a new politics around racial justice and identity. Drawing on the "Black is Beautiful" movement from the 1960s and 1970s and inspired in part by the continued work for racial justice in North and South America, Afro-Brazilians are proudly and publicly claiming their Black identities.

⏵ *If you have not yet, view the videos on the Black is Beautiful Movement avail-able in the section appendix.*

Over the past decade, the number of people identifying as Black or mixed race in Brazil has risen from 51% to 56% (McCoy and Trainao, 2020; Mitchell-Walthour, 2020). Afro-Brazilians are also running for political office.

In 2020, Afro-Brazilians made up 44% of city council seats nationwide (Mitchell-Walthour, 2020, para 5). The seeds for this movement have been planted and nurtured for many years. Miss Black Power Brazil is one example of the resistance, celebration, and activism that Afro-Brazilian women are leading.

In 2014 around Black Consciousness Day (November 20 annually), a group of Afro-Brazilian women organized a special event called Miss Black Power Brazil. More than a beauty competition, this event included scholars, writers, and artists who all came together to defy Eurocentric beauty standards, especially around hair; to educate younger generations; and to encourage Afro-Brazilian women to become politically active. The event began with a roundtable discussion with Afro-Brazilian writers and scholars.

> The contestants, who wore clothing by Black designers, had two things in common. They [were] politically active, and they [wore] their hair natural: without chemical straightener and with lots of volume, something that White standards of beauty in the mainstream media has discouraged Black women from doing in the past.
>
> (Osborn, 2014, para 3)

The winner, Maria Priscilla, was a literacy and Black history teacher in a low-income community in Rio de Janeiro. She said, "I see myself . . . as an activist, . . . bringing other references to my students: aesthetic, literary, and artistic references to tell the story of our people—so that these children know they have a story" (Osborn, 2014, para 13).

While Miss Black Power Brazil was a singular event, ripples of the work to center Afro-Brazilian voices, mobilize action, and redefine power and beauty standards continue in Brazil. And Afro-Brazilian women are leading the way (Mitchell-Walthour, 2020). In the 2020 election, Afro-Brazilian women won 14% of city council seats nationwide, up from just 3.9% of city council seats in the 2016 election (Mitchell-Walthour, 2020). As for beauty, in 2020, Raissa Santana was crowned Miss Brazil, the first Black woman to hold this title in 30 years (Scott, 2020).

Used with permission from Fishman-Weaver and Clingan, Teaching Women's and Gender Studies. Copyright © 2023, Taylor and Francis, Inc.

Artivism Lesson Notes (PCR)

Name_____ Date_____

	PRIOR KNOWLEDGE *What you already know*	CURIOSITIES *What you want to know*	RESEARCH *Questions and sources to explore*
Artivism			
Black is Beautiful Movement Related: #BlackGirlMagic			
Beauty and Power			

⏸ Take a Reflective Beat

- ◆ What inspired you in these two stories? What challenged you?
- ◆ How are identities, power, and beauty defined and redefined by the music of Las Krudas and events like Miss Black Power Brazil?
- ◆ Our focus word for this unit is *representation*. How are Las Krudas and Miss Black Power Brazil increasing representation?
- ◆ Share an example of another group, artist, or event that you admire for increasing representation and celebrating a multiplicity of voices and experiences.

Amanda Gorman, All Art Is Political

Amanda Gorman is the youngest inaugural poet in U.S. history. An award-winning writer and *cum laude* graduate of Harvard University, Gorman has performed at events for President Obama, President Biden, Lin-Manuel Miranda, Secretary Hillary Clinton, and Malala Yousafzai.

Take It for a Field Trip

Put some headphones on and either find a quiet place to listen to Gorman's TED talk "Using Your Voice is a Political Choice" or take it for a walk down the hall or around your school track. It is seven minutes long, and you may want to listen to it twice. After you've explored the talk on your own, meet up with three or four peers to discuss the following questions:

◆ Gorman states, "Poetry has never been the language of barriers; it's always been the language of bridges" (2:36). How do you think poetry can build bridges? What barriers could poetry knock down?
◆ Gorman believes that "All art is political" (3:14). How is art political? What are some examples of art being political (think about poetry or other literature, dance, visual arts, drama, etc.).
◆ At the beginning of her TED Talk, Gorman asks two questions: "One: Whose shoulders do you stand on? And two: What do you stand for?" (0:10). How would you answer those questions?

Community Poem

Brainstorm your answers to the two questions Amanda Gorman asked at the beginning of her TED Talk: Whose shoulders do you stand on? What do you stand for? Gorman answered those questions this way: "I am the daughter of Black writers, who are descended from Freedom Fighters who broke their chains and changed the world. They call me" (0:39).

You can use these sentence starters or create your own:

I stand on the shoulders of _____.
I stand for _____.

When you and your classmates have finished, stand in a circle. Take turns reading the first line around the circle, then the second. At the very end, read these lines in unison:

We are the children of our ancestors.
We stand for the stories only we can tell and for the change we will be in the world.

Used with permission from Fishman-Weaver and Clingan, Teaching Women's and Gender Studies. Copyright © 2023, Taylor and Francis, Inc.

Lesson 2: Vibrance, Belonging, and Trans Representation

Teaching Notes

As you prepare for this lesson, it may help to closely review Lesson 3—"'Two Spirit': Gender as a Social Construct" in Unit 1, including the teaching notes and care reminders. Before going through this lesson, review ground rules and norms that you have established with your scholars. (You can find example norms on pp. xx–xx.) If you haven't already done so, you may want to establish some specific ground rules related to gender-affirming language. This lesson requires a lot of unpacking, discovering, and listening. Giving your scholars permission to sit with an idea, to listen deeply, and to not have to respond right away (or at all) is powerful. Set the expectation that it is okay to say "pass" in these discussions. We all come to this lesson, as all lessons, with differing experiences and need different amounts of time to process. This diversity, not only of identity but also of how we learn and participate, is important.

Keeping Trans Youth Safe. Gender identity and trans representation are issues that have received a lot of attention recently. Much of this attention is negative, including legislation to limit and reduce trans rights, debates about access in sports and public facilities, and stories of violence against the trans community. Because of this attention, your LGBTQIA + scholars may be sorting through difficult emotions and experiences, including feeling unsafe and unwelcome in public or private spaces. Model compassion and care, recognizing that you and your scholars do not know everyone's lived experiences or identities. Further, because of this attention, some of your scholars may come to this lesson with strong preconceived notions. Encourage everyone to approach this lesson with an open mind and heart.

As you practice care in these lessons, pay particular attention to the scholars who have the most risk in these lessons. Whose stories are being told, and how are they being told? Seek every opportunity to affirm and celebrate your scholars, particularly your LGBTQIA+ scholars who may find mirror narratives in the following units. As you engage in this teaching, remember earlier reminders to check for joy. LGBTQIA+ histories, cultures, and identities are more than oppression and discrimination. They are also joy, art, leadership, innovation, and brilliance. Welcome scholars to a vibrant celebration of ideas and use these moments of joy to buoy your class in their ongoing pursuit of justice.

Review Vocabulary. Lesson 3—"'Two Spirit': Gender as a Social Construct" offered many vocabulary terms related to sex, gender, and gender-expansive identities. It may be helpful to review this vocabulary both on your own and with your scholars during this lesson.

Community Resources. If your school has a GSA (Genders and Sexualities Alliances or Gay-Straight Alliance) club, you may want to invite the club sponsor to visit your classroom to share additional information and educational resources.

Breaking the Binary. Later in the lesson, you and your scholars will explore short profiles of famous trans and nonbinary people who are making an impact in their field. For this activity, you may want to circle up the chairs in the room and read through the profiles together. You can even pass the book around if you like. Encourage scholars to take notes on interesting things they learn about the following key figures. You might put their names on the board before you start reading, so scholars can set up a notes sheet. Scholars can also share anything they already know about any of these key figures. As with all the lessons, we (Kathryn and Jill) also recommend showing images or videos of these key figures so that scholars can see the people we are studying.

- ◆ Rachel Levine—assistant secretary for health in the Department of Health and Human Services (United States)
- ◆ Geena Rocero—model, producer, activist (Philippines)
- ◆ Quinn—Olympic champion (Canada)
- ◆ Timothy DeLuc—figure skater (United States)
- ◆ Tanwarin Sukkhapisit—politician and filmmaker (Thailand)

 Thought Questions

- ◆ What would it look like to live in a gender-affirming world?
- ◆ How can we make our classrooms and schools more inclusive?

Through these lessons, you have learned about important human rights issues while exploring our three main themes of representation, resistance, and radical hope. Related to these themes are themes of belonging and celebration. This lesson addresses trans and nonbinary rights and representation and asks what it would be like to live in a gender-affirming world. Our current world is often not gender affirming, and this puts trans and nonbinary youth at risk. According to the Trevor Project's 2021 National Survey on LGBTQ Youth Mental Health:

- ◆ More than three of four transgender and nonbinary youth reported symptoms of generalized anxiety disorder.

◆ More than two of three transgender and nonbinary youth reported symptoms of major depression.
◆ More than half of trans and nonbinary youth considered committing suicide in 2020 (n.d.).

These statistics reflect an urgent crisis to keep trans and nonbinary youth safe.

Pronouns Matter

Term	Definition
Personal pronoun	A word that can be used to refer to someone in place of their name that indicates their gender identity. ◆ Examples include she/ella/him/they/zir.
Misgender	To refer to someone by a name, pronoun, or other identifier that is inconsistent with their gender or gender identity.

Has anyone ever mispronounced your name, misunderstood something you said, or assumed something about you that wasn't true? How did you feel in these situations? Although misgendering can happen to anyone, trans, gender non-binary, and gender-expansive individuals are often more misgendered and are even misgendered intentionally. Honoring and affirming everyone's full humanity is essential in cultivating a safe and inclusive world. This can start with something as simple as using the correct pronouns.

Using gender-affirming language improves mental health in the transgender community and reduces the risk of depression and even suicide. Here are some ways you can commit to gender-affirming language.

◆ When you introduce yourself, share your name and your pronouns. For example, I (Jill) might say, "Hi! I'm Jill. I go by she/her pronouns. It's nice to meet you!" This may feel a bit awkward at first, but it gets easier with time and opens the door for someone to share their pronouns with you if they wish. Likewise, you can include your pronouns on your nametags, email signatures, and social media profiles.
◆ If you do not know someone's gender or pronouns and cannot ask, use the person's name or refer to them by the gender-neutral pronouns "they/them."
◆ If someone uses pronouns that you are unfamiliar with, practice using the pronouns with a trusted friend until you get them right.
◆ If you hear someone misgender someone or use the incorrect pronouns, correct them. (This is important even if the person is not present.)

- ◆ If you make a mistake and accidentally call someone by the incorrect pronoun, apologize swiftly, correct your mistake, and make sure to use the correct pronouns later in the conversation.
- ◆ Avoid using unnecessary gendered or binary language (for example, use *friends* instead of *boys and girls* or *folks* instead of *guys*. Use *congressperson* instead of *congressmen* and *humankind* instead of *mankind*.)

Breaking Barriers

At the beginning of this lesson, you considered what it would look like to live in a gender-affirming world. How many things would have to change to make that vision a reality? In recent years, there have been powerful examples of both legislative forces and practices moving in tension both toward and away from a more inclusive and affirming world. This struggle reminds us that justice work is ongoing. Each act of courage and advocacy that helps break down barriers and expand inclusivity matters. Following are a few stories of transgender and nonbinary advocates working across sectors and boundaries toward a more affirming world.

Rachel Levine—Assistant Secretary for Health in the Department of Health and Human Services (United States)

Rachel Levine, the assistant secretary for health in the Department of Health and Human Services, is the first openly transgender person to be confirmed by the United States Senate. She was nominated by President Joe Biden and confirmed in March 2021. Levine understands firsthand the challenges and discrimination that individuals in the LGBTQIA+ community face in the health care system, and one of her goals as secretary for health and human services is to address this issue and empower LGBTQIA+ individuals in their medical care (Wamsley, 2021).

Geena Rocero—Model, Producer, Activist (Philippines)

Geena Rocero grew up in the Philippines and moved to the United States when she was 17. She became a U.S. citizen in 2006 (Rocero, 2015). She is a model, producer, and activist whose memoir about her story as a trans woman will be published 2023 (Tapp, 2021). She is also the director of *Caretakers*, a PBS documentary that tells stories of Filipino-American caretakers in the United States, including phlebotomist Angel Bonilla, who is the first transgender person to compete on the television show *The Voice* (PBS, 2021). Rocero uses her influence to bring awareness to Filipino and transgender issues and how they intersect.

Quinn—Olympic Champion (Canada)

In the 2020 Olympic Games in Tokyo, Canadian soccer player Quinn became the first transgender athlete to openly compete in the Olympics. Quinn is also the first transgender and nonbinary athlete to not only medal at the Olympics but also to win gold. Quinn's medal win was a huge win for inclusion and encouraging other trans and non binary young people as well. They hope to be a role model to inspire younger nonbinary athletes to play soccer (Pruitt-Young, 2021).

Timothy DeLuc—Figure Skater (United States)

In the 2022 Winter Olympics in Beijing, U.S. pairs figure skater Timothy DeLuc became the first openly nonbinary athlete to compete in an Olympic winter event. DeLuc and their partner, Ashley Cain-Gribble, are also making history as a pairs couple that does not conform to the stereotype of skating to romantic choreography that tells a story of a fragile feminine skater who is saved by her strong, masculine partner. Instead, they tell a different story of equality that breaks gender norms with their music, costumes, and skating style. DeLuc hopes that their success in this sport leads to a new narrative so that nonbinary athletes are free to be both open and successful. About their 2019 and 2022 U.S. Championship titles as well as their opportunity to compete in the Olympics, DeLuc said, "I think we want to dedicate these performances and this title to all the people that felt like they didn't belong—or were told that they didn't belong—in this sport" (Azzi, 2022).

Tanwarin Sukkhapisit—Politician and Filmmaker (Thailand)

A former English teacher, in 2019 Tanwarin Sukkhapisit became the first openly transgender member of parliament in Thailand's House of Representatives. Sukkhapisit is a kathoey (see Lesson 2 in Unit 1), and they represent the Future Forward Party. Before running for office, Sukkhapisit worked as a film director and actor focusing on short films that center the lived experiences of the LGBTQ+ community in Thailand. About their run for office, Sukkhapisit said,

> I want to write a new political history for Thailand. I spent years making films talking about the experience of transgender and LGBT people in Thailand but it no longer felt like enough to tell the story. I wanted to change the discriminatory laws.
>
> (Ellis-Petersen, 2019, para 4)

In 2020, Sukkhapisit was dismissed from their role in a controversial ruling. However, they are committed to continued work for gender justice. As the first to represent kathoey and the trans community in office, Sukkhapisit created space for more inclusive voices in government. By the time they were dismissed, three additional transgender representatives had been elected and remained in office.

Think, Pair, Share

◆ What surprised, challenged, or inspired you in reading these profiles?
◆ How is each person expanding representation in their field?
◆ What themes can you identify across these stories?
◆ If you could have lunch with one of these individuals, what would you want to talk about, ask them, or learn from their experiences?

Gender-Affirming School

In this next activity, consider how you can help create a safe, gender-affirming environment in your school. Like justice and wellness, this is an ongoing process. Start by recognizing the things your school community is already doing to affirm and include. How can you support those practices and further the cause of inclusion? Following are some resources you might consider: GSA club, local Free Mom Hugs chapter, LGBTQIA+ community or university center, school counselor, media specialists, school nurses, and your WGST classmates.

What Are Your Ideas for Creating a Gender-Affirming School?

◆

◆

◆

◆

Commit to one action that you will do yourself and brainstorm as a class something you can do as a group.

Exit Slip
To help make this school a gender-affirming space, I will _____ _____
To help make this school a gender-affirming space, we will _____ _____

Lesson 3: Disability Rights—Scholarship to Center and Celebrate Disability

 Thought Questions

◆ What would change if disability were viewed as an asset (strength)?
◆ Who are *your* role models from the disability community?
◆ What would it look like to live in a world that affirmed and celebrated (dis)abilities and differences?

In this lesson, you will explore how disability can be a strength, why neurodiversity is necessary in solving grand challenges, and how disability rights and advocacy are connected to the movements for a more just and inclusive world.

Term	Definition
Neurodiversity	The belief that differences and disabilities represent necessary and important variance in the human genome. Neurodiversity offers a strengths-based approach to disability and those who live, learn, perceive, and think differently.
Disability	In terms of legislative definitions, the Americans with Disabilities Act (ADA) and the Individuals with Disabilities Act (IDEA) shape most of the policy around disability in the United States. Disability is largely contextualized by the personal—and social—meanings that individuals ascribe to this identity. This means that families, teachers, and people with disabilities all have a lot of power to reconstruct how we understand disability. As one part of a child's identity, disability can contribute to specific strengths and challenges. Having a disability is both complex and limited in what it can (and can't) tell us. Further, disability is malleable; how it presents, the meanings we ascribe to it, and the significance it carries can all change over the course of an individual's life. (Fishman-Weaver, 2019)
Ableism	Discrimination against the disability community, including overt discrimination, erasing disabilities, casting disabilities as inherent deficits, and not creating accessible solutions or environments where all can thrive.

Term	Definition
Disability rights	A global social movement to expand access, rights, and opportunities to members of the disability community.
Universal design	Designing or reimagining a space, building, or organization to be as accessible and inclusive as possible. Universal design does not only benefit people with disabilities but can also improve the user experience for all. For example, consider how ramps help caregivers pushing strollers and how automatic doors help anyone carrying a heavy load.
People-first language	Language that puts the person before the disability, for example, *a person with autism*. People-first language emerged from disability rights work in the 1990s and purposefully pushed against outdated and deficit terms for talking about disability such as *handicapped*. People-first language is generally considered the most respectful option unless you know that an individual or community prefers a different convention, such as identity-first language (see next definition).
Identity-first language	In more recent years, some members of the disability community have advocated for identity-first language, for example, *autistic person*. This choice can center and celebrate a person's disability identity and their personhood. As with all identities, if you are unsure how a person would like to be referenced, ask. If you can't ask, err on the side of respect, dignity, and inclusion.

Approximately one billion people—or 15% of the global population—have a disability (World Health Organization, 2021). Yet the stories, accomplishments, and justice work of people from the disability community are too often missing from our histories, curricula, and media. People with disabilities are also often excluded or erased from feminist and social justice movements, and women of color are often further marginalized or missing altogether from these stories (Schalk and Kim, 2020).

Dr. Jina Kim is a researcher and professor in English Literature and Women's and Gender Studies at Smith College. She specializes in feminist disability studies and intersectionality related to race, gender, and disability. In alliance with other disability rights activists, Kim (2017) asks people to imagine what liberation (or freedom) would be like if "able-bodiedness is no longer centered" (para 4). Kim's work celebrates interdependence, collectives, vulnerability, and difference.

 Thought Question

◆ How do disability rights relate to your learning about more complete storytelling and justice work?

The neurodiversity movement explores these questions through cognitive differences. "Neurodiversity is a concept or movement that emphasizes that neurological differences should be recognized and respected as a variation of human wiring" (Amobi, 2021). Said another way, global challenges can't be solved without the creative and dedicated efforts of people who think differently.

Case Studies and Connections in Disability Rights—Class Jigsaw

Throughout this book, you have read about individuals who are rewriting inclusion and equity in purposeful ways. There have been stories of struggle and courage, stories of resistance and representation. The current running through these stories—and this book—is that of radical hope. With radical hope, individuals make courageous, intentional, and incremental changes and choices that build on each other to create the full story of change movements that move towards equity.

Activity Directions—In the following article jigsaw, you will read one case study on a disability rights activist. Take notes on the key points from the reading so that you can share in small groups with peers who have read other case studies. Just as each of these people is using their voices, art, passion, and professions to rewrite stories of inclusivism and equity, our worksheet also includes connecting activities for you to think about how your voice, passions, and art can make the world a better place.

Case Study 1—Maggie Aderin-Pocock: Space Scientist, Mechanical Engineer

Maggie Aderin-Pocock is a Black woman who was born in London to Nigerian parents. While she always loved math and science, Aderin-Pocock's dyslexia made reading and writing a struggle. She dreamed of going to space but worried whether her disability would make that dream impossible.

One day in science class, she knew the answer to a question that no one else did. This moment lit a spark of possibility, and Aderin-Pocock has been chasing and achieving her space dreams ever since. As a space scientist, she helped develop the Gemini telescope in Chili. As an activist for greater representation in science, she has met with more than 100,000 young people to show them that science, like feminism, is for everybody (The Yale Center for Dyslexia and Creativity, 2014).

She has said that because of her dyslexia, she "seemed to think different-ly from others in my group, and sometimes that can be so helpful because everybody's taking one route and you can say, 'Hold it. Have we considered this way or maybe we can go this way?'" (Made by Dyslexia, 2018, 2:07).

Aderin-Pocock did not overcome dyslexia; instead, she believes that because of her dyslexia, she has been given specific gifts including imagi-nation, storytelling, and empathy.

Case Study 2—Jessica Benham: Activist, Politician

Representative Jessica Benham shared in an interview that "People see themselves reflected in me, even when I'm not their rep. It is really cool" (Rouvalis, 2022, para 39). As both the first person with autism and first openly LGBTQIA+ person elected to the state legislature in Pennsylvania, Benham hopes to increase equity for individuals with disabilities and says, "I have been fighting my whole life to be heard and to ensure that other marginalized people are heard" (Budryk, 2019).

Elementary and secondary school were not easy for Benham, who had to repeat second grade and was often sent to the principal's office for dis-ruptive behavior. Like many women, she was not diagnosed with autism until she was in college (Rouvalis, 2022).[5] She draws directly on these experiences from her advocacy work as a state representative.

In a 2022 article in the *Pittsburgh Magazine*, Benham said,

> School systems are built to accommodate some kids but not other kids. In the early '90s, schools did not understand disability and difference and accommodation. It's not perfect now. We know that kids with disabilities and Black and brown kids are more often victims of school pushout. And I think because of my experience growing up, that's why I fight so hard on education issues.
>
> (Rouvalis, 2022, para 30)

Benham is known as a relationship builder even across the aisle and works alongside politicians who have very different views and experienc-es from her. In addition to being both queer and neurodiverse, Benham says people also connect with her because of her gender and age. At 30 years old, Benham is one of the youngest representatives.

Case Study 3—Annie Segara: Writer, Artist, YouTube Creator, Intersectional Activist

Following the Women's March in 2016, Annie Segara created the hashtag #thefutureisaccesible. This hashtag was a call to make feminism more inclusive and intersectional with respect to disabilities (Thompson, 2020).

Segara has both autism and Ehlers-Danlos syndrome, which is a connective tissue disorder that affects the skin, joints, and blood vessel walls. On her YouTube channel, where she is known as Annie Elainey, she shares videos about her lived experiences with disability, chronic illness, and being a queer Latinx creative. With a passion for storytelling, including multimedia stories, Segara advocates for body positivity and more inclusive stories. Other hashtags she has created and popularized include #AmbulatoryWheelchairUsersExist, #InvisiblyDisabledLooksLike, and #HotPersonInAWheelchair These hashtags invite more vibrant, celebratory, and inclusive stories to the media (Ngomsi, 2021).

Disability Rights Case Studies and Connections

Name_____ Date_____

Person	Key Points	Connection
Maggie Aderin-Pocock		**Spark Moments**—Getting that first right answer in science class was a spark moment or *inciting incident* for Aderin-Pocock. What are some important moments in your own life that have encouraged you to dream big?
Jessica Benham		**Your Identity Matters**—Representative Benham draws directly on her lived experiences to advocate for greater rights, access, and justice for members of the LGBTQ+ and disability communities. Your lived experiences give you invaluable knowledge, too. Create a personal crest on the aspects of your identity and culture that make you proud.
Annie Segara		**Make it Memorable**—Annie Segara has created a number of hashtags to draw attention to issues that matter deeply to her related to disability and gender rights. Create your own hashtag on an issue that matters deeply to you.

Used with permission from Fishman-Weaver and Clingan, Teaching Women's and Gender Studies. Copyright © 2023, Taylor and Francis, Inc.

An Affirming and Accessible School

Earlier in this lesson, you read about Annie Segara's creative work and hashtags that invite new and more inclusive stories. Another hashtag that has gained traction among the neurodiverse community is #actuallyautistic. This hashtag draws attention to the inherent expert knowledge people with autism have about autism; it also calls out people who attempt to speak on behalf of a disability or identity they don't have. As we close this lesson, consider what you and your peers could do to cultivate a disability affirming and accessible school. Be specific and strengths-based in your suggestions. Remember the message of #actuallyautistic[6] as well as our earlier work about humanizing research and rejecting savior narratives. Review the thought questions from the beginning of this lesson and then develop some plans with your peers to cultivate a disability affirming and more accessible school.

How Will You and Your Peers Cultivate a Disability Affirming and Accessible School?

- ◆
- ◆
- ◆
- ◆

Review your list and star one action that you (or your class) will commit to working toward this week.

Lesson 4: The Ripple Effect of Being First—Representation in Government

This lesson explores gender representation in leadership, particularly government, and the ripple effect of being first. While you might not be running for a political office just yet, you may have already had moments when you were the first from your family or a cultural or identity group to step into a new space or role.

(▶) As you and your classmates explore these themes, watch the interview with Amanda Gorman for the Today Show. A link to this interview is in the appendix. You have read and heard many examples of Amanda Gorman's powerful work throughout these lessons. In this interview, she talks about being the first youth poet laureate in the United States. As you watch, consider these questions:

- ◆ What responsibility does Gorman feel as not only the first person to hold this position but also as the first woman and the first person of color?
- ◆ How does this interview connect to our earlier lessons on race, identity, gender, and disability?
- ◆ Who and what does she say inspires her?
- ◆ If you were being interviewed on stepping boldly into a new position, one that no one has ever held, what position would you hope for? If asked, who or what would say inspired you?

Global Snapshot—A Long Way to Go Toward Gender Parity in Government

The United Nations cites "women's equal participation and leadership in political and public life" as "essential to achieving the Sustainable Development Goals" (UN Women, 2021a). Leadership in the highest office in government is not the only measure of gender equality and progress; however, it is an important issue in our global work toward sustainability, prosperity, and inclusion. Of the 195 nations in the world, only 70 have elected a woman leader, and only five of the ten most populous countries have elected a woman to lead their country (Encyclopedia Britannica, 2020). While there are important cultural differences in how leaders are selected for the highest office in government (e.g. appointment, democratic election), women continue to be underrepresented at all levels of decision-making worldwide (UN Women, n.d.-b). Women of color, LGBTQIA+ individuals, women with disabilities, Indigenous women, and women from lower income backgrounds are even further underrepresented in top leadership positions.

Term	Definition
Gender parity	The equal participation and representation of genders within an organization, position, or population. Achieving gender parity in the highest levels of government would mean that as many women serve in these highest offices as do men.

In September 2021, there were only 26 women serving as heads of state. "At the current rate, gender equality in the highest positions of power will not be reached for another 130 years" (UN Women-n.d.-a, n.d.-b). As Women's and Gender Studies scholars, we want to:

◆ analyze the forces and barriers that contribute to this systemic under representation of women in top leadership positions,
◆ celebrate the bravery and impact of those leaders who were the first from their identity or cultural group to step into specific roles, and
◆ explore the conditions (ripples) created by these important "firsts" and the potential for continued progress and positive change.

On Whose Shoulders? An Abridged U.S Government Lesson (1965–2022)

On January 20, 2021, Kamala Harris was sworn in as first woman vice president of the United States. During her speech to accept her vice presidential nomination, she said, "While I may be the first woman in this office, I won't be the last" (Read Vice-President Elect Kamala Harris' Full Victory Speech, 2020). In this activity, we will explore a timeline of firsts that led up to this historic moment. Before we do, discuss these questions with a partner:

◆ What does it mean to be a leader?
◆ Who are the women leaders in your community?
◆ Why is it important to understand historical firsts?

In her acceptance speech, Harris specifically honored the women of color whose shoulders she stood on to reach this position. We list some of them next, as well as other significant firsts for women both before and after her appointment. While the United States has yet to have a woman president, the list below focuses on historic firsts for women in U.S. federal government positions including top elected and appointed positions.

Teaching Notes

In this activity, scholars will explore historical firsts in the U.S. Government. This activity has several steps to guide scholars through their learning. Completing the entire activity may take a few class periods.

In preparation, you will want to photocopy the historical figures timeline. You will need two copies of this document. Cut one document into strips, so that each event/date is on its own strip. Save the other copy to project later.

Scholar Directions

- ◆ Step 1: Draw a slip from the timeline.
- ◆ Step 2: Find peers who have the same role as yours. Examples include representative, senator, Supreme Court justice, presidential nominee, vice president, and Cabinet position. As a team, research the duties of that position.
- ◆ Step 3: Beginning with 1965, organize yourselves in chronological order. Take one step apart for each year. (Hint: You might complete this activity outside.)
- ◆ Step 4: Read the timeline aloud. Practice projecting your voice.
- ◆ Step 5: Come back together as a class and share what you noticed.
- ◆ Step 6: Project the timeline on the board so the class can look at it together.
- ◆ Step 7: Complete the 3–2–1 directions below.
- ◆ Step 8: Share your Google Slide presentation with the class.

Expanding Gender Representation in the U.S. Government—Key Historical Figures

1965	Patsy Takemoto Mink became the first Asian Pacific Islander to be elected to the U.S. House of Representatives.
1969	Shirley Chisholm became the first Black woman elected to the U.S. House of Representatives.
1977	Mary Rose Oakar became the first Middle Eastern/North African woman to be elected to the U.S. House of Representatives.
1981	Sandra Day O'Connor became the first woman to serve as a Supreme Court justice.
1984	Geraldine Ferraro became the first woman on a vice presidential ticket during Walter Mondale's campaign for presidency.
1993	Carol Moseley Braun, a Black woman, became the first woman of color to be elected to the U.S. Senate.
1993	Janet Reno became the first woman attorney general of the United States.
1993	Ruth Bader Ginsburg was appointed as the first Jewish woman to serve as a U.S. Supreme Court justice.
1997	Madeleine Albright became the first woman secretary of state.
1997	Loretta Sanchez became the first Latina to be elected to the U.S. House of Representatives.
2007	Nancy Pelosi became the first woman Speaker of the House.
2009	Sonia Sotomayor became the first Latina United States Supreme Court justice.
2012	Mazie Hirono became the first Asian-Pacific woman to be elected to the U.S. Senate.
2016	Hillary Clinton became the first woman presidential nominee on a major political party ticket.
2017	Tammy Duckworth (Asian Pacific Islander), Catherine Cortez Masto (Latina), and Kamala Harris (Black and South Asian) were elected to the United States Senate, all historic firsts for their racial and gender identities.
2021	Kamala Harris was sworn in as first woman vice president of the United States.
2021	Rachel Levine became the first transgender person for a Senate-confirmed post when President Biden appointed her the assistant secretary of health (Cabinet position).

Used with permission from Fishman-Weaver and Clingan, Teaching Women's and Gender Studies. Copyright © 2023, Taylor and Francis, Inc.

2021	Debra Haaland became the first Native American to serve in the president's cabinet when she was confirmed secretary of the interior (Cabinet position). In 2019, she became the first Native American/Alaskan Native woman to be elected to the U.S. House of Representatives.
2021	Avril Haines became the first woman to serve as director of national intelligence (Cabinet position).
2021	Janet Yellin, who made history as the first woman to chair the Federal Reserve from 2014 to 2018, became the first woman to serve as treasury secretary (Cabinet position).
2022	Ketanji Brown Jackson was appointed as the first Black woman to serve as a U.S. Supreme Court justice.

Used with permission from Fishman-Weaver and Clingan, Teaching Women's and Gender Studies. Copyright © 2023, Taylor and Francis, Inc.

Reflective Learning—Connecting to an Historic First

Name_____ Date_____

After you have read through the timeline on expanding gender representation in the U.S. Federal Government, fill out this 3–2–1 chart to reflect on your experience.

3	What are three things you learned that you didn't know before? 1. 2. 3.
2	What are two trends or observations you notice about the possible ripple effect of firsts? 1. 2.
1	Who is one key figure in this timeline that you would like to learn more about? 1.

Create a Google Slide Presentation

Research one of the key figures from this lesson or another of your choosing and create a Google Slides presentation. Use one slide to address each bullet point.

◆ Who is this key figure? (Explain their role, their background, and key accomplishments.)
◆ On whose shoulders do they stand? (Explain the historical context and any primary influences on this person's work.)
◆ How did this person's work advance justice, equality, and representation?
◆ What connections can you make between your own lived experiences and your research on this key figure?

Used with permission from Fishman-Weaver and Clingan, Teaching Women's and Gender Studies. Copyright © 2023, Taylor and Francis, Inc.

Take a Reflective Beat

In this lesson, we explored famous firsts. However, this list is incomplete on several levels, including state and local government, firsts from countries outside the United States, and firsts in other sectors besides government.

◆ What other firsts would you like to research?
◆ Why does representation matter, in leadership, government, and our daily lives?

Unit 6—From Our Ancestors: Change Movements for a More Just World

Throughout these lessons, you and your scholars have considered ancestral knowledge, the wisdom of our elders, and the power of more complete histories. Through a weighty guiding question, we return to these themes in this closing unit. That question is: Is it possible to right equity wrongs? This question requires scholars to understand equity and to make claims about what it would be like to take an injustice and make it right.

The unit begins by studying Claudette Colvin. Nine months before Rosa Parks' powerful act of resistance, Ms. Colvin also refused to give up her seat on a segregated bus in Montgomery, Alabama. She, too, acted out of purpose, having just learned about Sojourner Truth and Harriet Tubman in school. She was arrested, but unlike Rosa Parks, history did not cast her story as heroic. That didn't stop Ms. Colvin from continuing to work for racial justice and civil rights and from making a significant difference. However, she did so with a criminal record that called her a "juvenile delinquent." Sixty-six years later, on December 16, 2021, a judge finally expunged her record and apologized.

Next we study Ms. Opal Lee, who is known as the grandmother of Juneteenth. As a middle schooler, Ms. Lee saw her home set on fire and ransacked by white supremacists. The date of the attack, June 19th, is a significant date in United States history as it celebrates the end of African American enslavement. The attackers chose this date strategically, but the Lee family persisted. In her 80s, Ms. Lee laced up her sneakers and went on a walking mission across the United States to get Juneteenth recognized as a national holiday. Under the Biden administration, she won. Ms. Lee didn't stop there. She is now in her 90s and continuing to work for racial justice in Texas.

Ms. Colvin and Ms. Lee changed the course of U.S. policy and legislation. They deserve a place in our history books, and we (Kathryn and Jill) are proud that their stories are included. However, we are also committed to celebrating the everyday stories of ancestors who may not have been invited to the White House, whose stories are not found on CNN or the BBC but whose legacy lives on in each of us. In the next lesson, scholars will learn about Marília Mascarenhas. She is the grandmother to high school student Matheus Nucci Mascarenhas, and he tells us that her stories of growing up in Brazil inspire him to work toward greater gender justice.

This unit closes by asking scholars to practice radical hope in authoring their own policy proposal. The policy they choose can be small, such as a norm or rule in the classroom that they believe is standing in the way of inclusion. Small incremental changes can be transformative. The policy they choose can be larger, something in their city politics that they present to city council, or even a proposal for their state representatives. Perhaps they will lace up their metaphorical (or literal) shoes like Ms. Opal Lee and pound the pavement for justice. Perhaps they will draw on their own heroes from their Women's and Gender Studies lessons like Ms. Colvin. Perhaps, like Matheus, they will sit down with their own grandparents for inspiration and guidance. However your scholars choose to advance justice, to affirm humanity, and to expand access and opportunity, we (Kathryn and Jill) believe our communities and ultimately the world will be better for their leadership.

Key Term: *Radical Hope*

Radical hope is about facing situations with eyes wide open for challenges and injustices, committing to problem-solving through a values-based framework, and ultimately believing that schools and by proxy communities can be more just and humane places.

In 2018, I (Kathryn) developed this concept while doing research on gendered organizational theory in school leadership. Drawing on radical, liberal, and postmodern feminisms, I wanted to explore how schools could be sites for justice, inclusion, and change. From radical feminisms, I asked what needed to be deconstructed and rebuilt completely in another way. From liberal feminisms, I asked questions about representation and policy. How could we work within systems to improve them? From postmodern feminisms, I asked questions about discourse and social construction. What do we mean by *school, teacher, leader,* and *learner* and how could those definitions be reimagined?

In my own work in schools, it is a concept I kept returning to. These same questions guided our work when we engaged in an equity and representation audit of our curriculum. It was central to our *core values* work with my school leadership team. It's also been a light on my porch when offering care and trying to make sense of global issues and humanitarian crises, most recently when visiting with a Ukrainian family about the war. As sometimes happens when a fledgling concept flies out in the world, this one has gained strength and nuance. It has been a tethering concept in my last two research projects, first on connected and series teaching (co-authored with Stephanie Walter) and now on this book with Jill.

Radical hope has three main guideposts:

- ◆ An honest and critical look at injustices as a playbook for what needs to change or be changed.
- ◆ An honest and celebratory look at justices as a playbook for what needs to be cultivated and centered.
- ◆ A belief that a better, more just, and more humane community, organization, or relationship is possible and a commitment to keep working toward that reality.

Radical hope calls out injustice and works with purpose toward justice, inclusion, access, and belonging.

Lesson 1: Is It Possible to Right Equity Wrongs?

 Thought Questions

- Create a list of the major social injustices of our time.
- Who and which communities have been harmed by these injustices?
- What would it look like to heal and repair these injustices?
- How long is too long to wait for justice?

In this lesson, you will learn about Claudette Colvin and Opal Lee, two women who have worked for justice for decades. Both are dedicated to expanding civil rights and racial justice. Both also experienced traumatic and defining events in their early teenage years. Their stories teach us that you are never too old or too young to make a difference and that justice work is ongoing.

Claudette Colvin, the Teenager Who Helped Desegregate Montgomery Busses

Charges Expunged 66 Years Later

Nine months before Rosa Parks' act of resistance led to the Montgomery Bus boycott, 15-year-old Claudette Colvin refused to give up her seat on a segregated bus in Montgomery, Alabama. Black History Month had just ended, and Colvin and her classmates had been studying important Black leaders like Harriet Tubman and Sojourner Truth. Colvin said it was her constitutional right to keep the seat she had paid for (Begnaud and Reardon, 2021). She was handcuffed and arrested, and the case was heard in juvenile court, where a judge declared that Colvin was a "delinquent" and placed her on probation "as a ward of the state pending good behavior."

She continued to work for civil rights and was a plaintiff in the landmark lawsuit that outlawed racial segregation on Montgomery's buses. However, even after the law was overturned, Ms. Colvin never heard that her probation was complete. She waited and never got in any trouble. She kept waiting. Sixty-six years later, in 2021, a judge finally expunged her record.[7]

Ms. Colvin said that although she is now an elderly woman, clearing her name will matter to her children, her grandchildren, and Black children everywhere. She said,

> When I think about why I'm seeking to have my name cleared by the state, it is because I believe if that happened it would show the

generation growing up now that progress is possible, and things do get better. It will inspire them to make the world better.

(Associated Press, 2021, para 10)

▶ **Watch the video "Civil Rights Pioneer Claudette Colvin Has Arrest Records Expunged."** You can find a link in our chapter appendix. Following the video, share your reactions to the following questions.

◆ What surprised you in this video?
◆ Who are the heroes in this story? Defend your answer. Note: There are multiple answers to this question.
◆ What does Ms. Colvin's story teach us about the importance of teaching and celebrating Black History and Women's History?
◆ What is Claudette Colvin's legacy, and how will you honor that legacy?

Opal Lee, the Grandmother of Juneteenth

The difference between Juneteenth and the 4th of July? Woo, girl! The fact is none of us are free till we're all free.

—Opal Lee[8]

Opal Lee, a retired elementary school teacher and grandmother, made history when she inspired U.S. President Joe Biden to name Juneteenth a national holiday. Opal Lee had fond memories of celebrating Juneteenth, but her commitment to making this day a national holiday extended far behind the festivities. She also carries the memories of a harrowing Juneteenth that left a deep scar. In 1939, when Ms. Lee was 13 years old, an angry mob of white supremacists set her house on fire and ransacked their family home. Her family had recently moved to a predominantly White neighborhood, and the message that they weren't welcome was overwhelming.

Term	Definition
Juneteenth	Juneteenth is considered the longest standing African American holiday and is often celebrated with festivals, food, music, and heritage. The history of this important day begins in 1863 with Abraham Lincoln's Emancipation Proclamation declaring that all enslaved people be set free. Two and a half years later on "Juneteenth" (June 19, 1865), federal troops stormed Galveston, Texas, to enforce the emancipation proclamation. More than 250,000 people were freed as a result of these actions. Galveston, Texas, was considered to be the last place in the United States not observing Lincoln's declaration. Six months after Juneteenth, the 13th Amendment was passed, which constitutionally outlawed human enslavement.

In 2016, Ms. Lee made it her mission to make Juneteenth a national holiday. She was 89 years old at the time when she started a mission to walk from her home in Fort Worth, Texas, to the United States Capitol in Washington, D.C. She walked in 2.5-mile increments, commemorating the 2.5 years it took for the federal troops to arrive in Galveston following the emancipation. Along the way, she stopped and gave talks and met with students. As a school teacher, counselor, and activist, Ms. Lee has a long commitment to education and antiracist teachings. Ms. Lee has been adamant in interviews that while she walked hundreds of miles, she didn't walk the whole route from Fort Worth to Washington, D.C. Still, her mission drew local and national attention; some celebrities, including Sean "Diddy" Combs, Lupita Nyong'o, and Usher, even got involved (Associated Press, 2021). The racial justice movements of the summer of 2020 brought Juneteenth into mainstream spotlights, and more people took up the cause of teaching the history of this important day in United States history and joining in the celebration.

(▶) Watch the White House video of Ms. Lee recounting the signing of the bill that made Juneteenth a national holiday.

In these units, you have explored how justice work is ongoing. Few people embody this with more vigor than Ms. Opal Lee. After Juneteenth became a federal holiday, Ms. Lee laced up her sneakers and got right back to work. In 2022, at 95 years old, Ms. Opal Lee continues working for justice. A few of her other initiatives include helping to establish the Tarrant County Black Historical & Genealogical Society, which preserves and tracks Fort Worth's Black history; founding Citizens Concerned with Human Dignity, which is aimed at helping Fort Worth's economically disadvantaged; supporting a local nonprofit to acquire a former KKK meeting hall on 1012 Main St. and transforming it into a center for multicultural healing and arts; and starting the Fort Worth Juneteenth Museum, which will become the National Juneteenth Museum and is intended to open in 2023. These efforts were recently recognized in her nomination for a Nobel Peace Prize (Rivas, 2022).

Think, Pair, Share

- ◆ What surprised, challenged, or inspired you in this story?
- ◆ What are the most important lessons we learn from Ms. Lee's work?
- ◆ What is Opal Lee's legacy, and how will you honor that legacy?

Exit Slip: Reparations

Term	Definition
Reparations	To make right or repair: the making of amends for a wrong one has done by resources or other tangible support to those who have been wronged.

In the United States, activists have debated what reparations might look like for the descendants of human enslavement and the violent colonization of Indigenous people. Reparations can also happen on a smaller scale.

Translated from Hebrew, *Tikkun Olam* means roughly to heal, repair, and transform the world. As we close this lesson, respond to the following questions.

- ◆ What was healed, repaired, or transformed through the work of Claudette Colvin and Opal Lee?
- ◆ What injustices have you observed in your community?
- ◆ How will you commit to healing, repairing, and transforming these injustices?

Lesson 2: Lessons From Our Grandmothers' Change Movements

Shortly after Jill and I (Kathryn) started working on this book, I visited my maternal grandmother. I am incredibly fortunate to still have regular four-generation "girls' weekends" with my grandma, mother, daughter, and myself. During this particular visit, my daughter (age 10) was telling her great grandmother about *this feminist book her mom was writing*. My grandma smiled and nodded. She asked my daughter what she wanted to do when she grew up.

My daughter hesitated and then said, "Well, I am not sure if I want to be a veterinarian, an environmental lawyer, or an animal science researcher."

My grandma leaned in close:

> You have so many options now. You can do so many things. Do them all. Do anything you want to do. When I was young, my choices were secretary, nurse, or teacher. Things are different now. You have so many directions to choose from.

As authors, educators, and mothers, Jill and I believe that the lessons of our ancestors continue to inform our contemporary work toward gender justice. Throughout this book, we have encouraged you to learn from your grandmothers (if possible) and those who came before. In our own work teaching Women's and Gender Studies with middle and high school scholars, we have seen how these conversations can be both didactic and transformative. Matheus Nucci Mascarenhas was a high school junior at our school when he interviewed his grandmother, Marília Mascarenhas (age 77). We found this interview so relevant to this book that we asked for his and his grandmother's permission to include the excerpts and reflections printed below.[9]

Women's Rights and Gender Equality in the 1960s in Brazil

Guest Contributor: Matheus Nucci Mascarenhas

The interview with my grandmother, Marília Mascarenhas, expanded my understanding of the feminist movements throughout history. Her testimonial is engaging as it depicts the reality of many women who lived decades ago, in the 1960s.

Matheus: How do you think society's cultural patterns restricted your vocational aspirations?

Marília: Worst of all, in my opinion, was not even the salary difference, but the inability of women to achieve the same positions as men. . . . For example, I worked as a secretary for a long time of my life, and, in fact, I devoted myself remarkably to work. . . . However, as I watched my husband get promoted several times in the company, my position had remained the same for many years, even though I constantly demonstrated proficiency and excellence in many aspects of working life. . . . And I can say this with great conviction, since I, like my husband, have an academic diploma at a university, in the course of language, at one of the best universities in Brazil. . . . But even so, the opportunities I had at that time in the 60s were limited.

Matheus: Have you ever faced discrimination of gender in the workplace or in a public space?

Marília: This is a sensitive subject. . . . One striking moment of discrimination was when I was riding a bike to college, wearing jeans. . . . At that time, this was unusual, but I wore them anyway as I thought they were gorgeous. I always noticed a few crooked looks when I wore pants, but nothing that would bother me. . . . However, there was one day when I was walking past the old square of the Rosario in the center of Belo Horizonte, when a young man, along with some friends, started whistling at me and shouting: "Hey you lady, take off those men's pants and show me what's underneath." And he started laughing really loud with his friends, mocking me and screaming. . . . That day, I was so, so embarrassed that I didn't dare wear my pants and go that way for a long, long time. . . . When I tell it like this, it seems like a lie, as it is so absurd, but evil exists everywhere. And this episode of discrimination or, as we can say today, of *sexual harassment*, is something that was very important to me, as it taught me to value myself and to fight the mediocrities of these nasty men. So much so that soon after, I participated in three or four demonstrations, which, among various agendas, had the rights of women as one of the headlines. . . .

Matheus: Tell what the feminist social movements in the 1960s in Brazil were like and if you have ever participated in marches and demonstrations regarding that topic.

Marília: In college, right after the incident of discrimination I told you about earlier, some friends invited me to a group of young people who were going to protest. Among the agendas was the increase of women's rights. . . . During this period, we were in a military dictatorship in Brazil, which throughout its extension, was repressive and aggressive to all those who were against it. . . . We then organized this demonstration to take place on the main avenue in Belo Horizonte. . . . On the day, thousands of young people gathered with "down the dictatorship" and "women have power" posters in the walk to the central square. When I took part in the demonstration, no violence happened. . . . However, some colleagues told me that at the end of the day, soldiers beat them with clubs in the square and began to dissolve the demonstrators brutally. . . . Anyway, after this march, I sometimes participated in leafleting and some smaller demonstrations.

Marília's Concluding Thoughts

Women's rights are very important for the development of society and therefore must be taken seriously. I express my support for the movements that struggle daily for transformations. Thank you so much for this interview, my dear grandson!

Matheus's Concluding Thoughts

The transformations brought by the tireless struggles of the feminist waves have modified our social framework and altered the sexist mechanisms of society. Although the path for ideal gender equality is still challenging and lengthy, a social transformation has arrived and continues to come. During the 1960s and 1970s, brave women organized rallies, events, marches, and speeches to bring awareness of equality. Their tenacity to address gender inequality improved women's representation in prestigious job positions, politics, and in academic environments. Moreover, these women brought about change when increasing access to equal education, equal pay, and reproductive rights. Nowadays, what is still lacking for the feminist movement is the capacity to alter not just the law and the rights but also the people's sexist mentality. My grandmother's voice is strong. This interview showed me the perspective of a progressive woman who intended to propel practical changes to further the cause of gender equality.

Reflection Questions

◆ What did you learn in this interview with Marília Mascarenhas? Consider both her own story and what she shared about the political context of Brazil in the 1960s.

◆ In Concept I, many of you interviewed an elder in your family or community. Compare and contrast this interview with that interview. If you did not do the interview, think of other conversations you have had with your grandmothers or women from previous generations. What similarities, differences, and key takeaways can you identify?

◆ In this unit, we are studying change movements. How can you see change or change movements occurring in this interview?

◆ What lessons and themes from our WGST studies can you identify in this narrative?

Exit Slip: On Tenacity

Matheus ends his interview with his grandmother with a reflection on tenacity. Tenacity is often associated with persistence or determination; it means to hold tight to something and commit. Complete this sentence as an exit slip for this lesson.

I have a tenacity for justice.

This looks like _____.
This sounds like _____.
This feels like_____.
For me, this means _____.

Lesson 3: Policy Proposal—A Catalyst for Justice

Term	Definition
Policy	A norm, rule, law, or course of action required by an organization, government, business, group, or individual. The four types of policies include public policy, organizational policy, functional policy, and specific policy.

✔ Quick Check for Understanding

Several of the activists we have studied in these last two units affected policy change.

What policies did the following activists, representatives, and advocates help inform?

Person	Policies and Impact
Rachel Levine	
Claudette Colvin	
Opal Lee	
The key figure you researched in Lesson 4, "The Ripple Effect of Being First"	
Jessica Benham	

In Unit 1, you explored the following definition of feminism: "An affirmation of humanity that seeks freedom from oppression and commits to the full access of social, health, economic, and political rights and opportunities for all people." In Unit 2, you considered this question: How can fairness, equity, and a "love ethic" affirm humanity and free people from oppression (CNN—bell hooks, 2020)? In this final lesson, you will explore how policy change can be one tool for advancing this vision in your class, school, city, or state. However, before you begin drafting your own policy proposal, we want to explore the work of one more expert in this area—former Supreme Court Justice Ruth Bader Ginsburg.

"Women Belong in All Places Where Decisions Are Made[10]"—RBG's Career to Transform Gender Justice in the United States

Former Supreme Court Justice Ruth Bader Ginsburg is a powerful role model for advancing gender justice through policy change. Ruth Bader Ginsburg was the second woman to serve on the U.S. Supreme Court, a role she held until her passing in 2021 at age 87. As a Jewish woman, Justice Ginsburg experienced marginalization throughout her career and drew on these experiences to expand justice for marginalized groups. During her studies at Harvard Law School, Ginsburg was one of nine women. Ginsburg was known for being a fierce researcher, a methodical advocate on behalf of gender justice, and a relationship builder including relationships with stakeholders who held very different beliefs than hers. She also strategically represented men in gender justice cases showing that gender equity affects all people. You'll read more about this strategy in the Mortiz example described next. What follows is a list of seven landmark cases that Ginsburg worked on during her career to expand gender justice and equity.

Name_____ Date_____

SEVEN LANDMARK CASES THAT JUSTICE RUTH BADER GINSBURG WORKED ON DURING HER CAREER		
Year	**Decision**	**Background**
1968	We can all be caregivers.	Ginsburg represented Charles Mortiz, a single man who cared for his elderly mother. Mortiz had been denied a caregiver tax deduction because he was both unmarried and a man. Ginsburg's representation determined that the IRS had violated the Equal Protection Clause of the U.S. Constitution, and in 1971, Section 214 of the IRS Code was amended to expand caregiving deductions regardless of sex. This case opened the door for a powerful list of policy changes eliminating discrimination "on the basis of sex" (Rodriguez, 2020).
1974	Expanded economic rights	Ginsburg's work was important for the Equal Credit Opportunity Act (1974), which gave women the right to apply for bank accounts, credit cards, and mortgages without a male co-signer.
1979	Protections for pregnant employees	Ginsburg worked with Susan Deller Ross to pass the Pregnancy Discrimination Act (1979), which made it so that employers could not discriminate against employees based on gender or reproductive choices.
1979	More representative juries	Ginsburg has famously said, "Women belong in all places where decisions are being made" (Biskupik, 2009). In 1979, her work led to a change in jury laws saying that women were also required to serve on juries.
1996	Expanded educational opportunities	Ginsburg led the decision in the *United States v. Virginia* (1996) that said schools that receive state funding must admit women. This case began with the Virginia Military Institute and then, as in so many of her decisions, gave way to a positive ripple of greater access and gender inclusion.
2015	Marriage rights	Ginsburg voted with the majority opinion in a 5–4 ruling on *Obergefell v. Hodges*, which drew on the Fourteenth Amendment to expand marriage equality to same-sex couples. Ginsburg was also the first justice to conduct same-sex marriages.

Used with permission from Fishman-Weaver and Clingan, Teaching Women's and Gender Studies. Copyright © 2023, Taylor and Francis, Inc.

Year	Decision	Background
2020	Expanded protections for queer employees	One of Ginsburg's final cases was *Bostock v. Clayton County* in 2020. Bostock had been fired from his job shortly after expressing interest in a gay softball league. Queer identities were not previously covered under the Civil Rights Act. However, this case challenged that claim and ruled in favor of Bostock, therefore protecting gay, transgender, and queer employees against work discrimination. Ginsburg again voted with the majority on this landmark case.

I Dissent! There were many cases in Ginsburg's career, including during her work with the Supreme Court, that did not go the way she wanted. In several of these instances, Ginsburg exercised her power of dissent by delivering and recording powerful texts that outlined her principled beliefs on the issues at hand.

Storybook Page—Working in small teams, create a storybook page summarizing one of the key cases discussed. Your page should include descriptions and illustrations appropriate for early elementary children. Book pages should answer the questions:

◆ What was the decision?
◆ Why did it matter?

As always, creativity is encouraged!

Exit Question: What is Justice Ginsburg's legacy?

Used with permission from Fishman-Weaver and Clingan, Teaching Women's and Gender Studies. Copyright © 2023, Taylor and Francis, Inc.

You Can Be a Catalyst for Justice

One of the strategies Justice Ginsberg used is specificity. She chose very specific cases that she believed in and fought with smarts and vigor. These cases often had positive ripples and ramifications for greater justice well beyond her initial clients. As you and your peers brainstorm for your policy proposal, practice specificity. What is a small change you would like to see in your classroom, school, or local community? Why does this change matter to you and your peers? Throughout these units, you have learned about the ways discrimination and oppression are often rooted within systems and organizations. Rewriting policy is one way to reconstruct our systems and calibrate them toward a more just and affirming reality. Over the next few days, pay attention to the ways policy impacts you and your peers. Report back to your peer policy groups on what you notice. Then choose a specific cause to take up. You might propose a rewriting of an existing policy, or you might propose something entirely new. After you have chosen your issue, use the policy proposal outline to begin drafting.

This work has the potential to transform your communities and local practices. Don't let it just sit in your notebooks or get forgotten as another school assignment. Finalize your proposals and find a way to present them to key stakeholders. This might look like a meeting with your school administrative team, a presentation to your city council or school board, or meeting with your state representatives. Your voice and your ideas matter. In fact, they may be the next great catalyst toward a more just and inclusive community. Thank you for your dreams and your leadership.

Name_____

Date_____

POLICY PROPOSAL OUTLINE

Introduction

◆ What issue, challenge, or injustice is your proposed policy attempting to solve? Be specific. Appeal to your stakeholder's sense of both logic (logos) and emotion (pathos).

◆ Are there any current policies related to this issue? If so, why are they insufficient?

Summary

◆ How will your policy help solve the problem? Again, be specific. What will be the impact of this new policy?

◆ Who are the stakeholders affected by this issue and policy?

◆ How does this policy relate to existing laws, rules, mission statements, or values?[11]

Logistics

◆ How will you educate others about this policy?

◆ How will the policy be implemented and enforced?

Here are a few ideas for spreading the word about your policy proposal. Write a letter for your local newspaper (e.g. letter to the editor), speak to local government or school officials, host a teach-in at school, or write your congressperson or give a testimony in your state capitol. You and your team may have more ideas as well!

Used with permission from Fishman-Weaver and Clingan, Teaching Women's and Gender Studies.
Copyright © 2023, Taylor and Francis, Inc.

Name_____ **Date**_____

Course Synthesis Project: Toward Justice and Joy

Task. Drawing on your unique body of Women's and Gender Studies work and your personal passions and experiences, create a project that showcases your learning, calls others to action, and moves us toward justice and joy. This project should play to your unique strengths (e.g. art, writing, speaking, video, graphic design). No two synthesis projects will be the same because no two scholars are the same. In this activity, we celebrate the unique and varied experiences, interests, and interpretations you bring to this work.

Background. In these lessons, you have read how Women's and Gender Studies (WGST) calls us to:

◆ think critically across disciplines and points of view;
◆ offer and celebrate more complete stories of history, culture, and identity;
◆ affirm a multiplicity of lived experiences and perspectives; and
◆ work to further the cause of justice and equity while also reducing oppression and marginalization.

In this final synthesis project, you will demonstrate your scholarship and leadership to do each of these things. Your project will be unique to you and your constellation of identities, experiences, strengths, and passions. You may even draw on the dreams or wisdom of your ancestors.

You have planned research and action projects and engaged in art, narrative, writing, and scholarship. You may further develop one of your works in progress or create something brand new that synthesizes your most important takeaways from these lessons.

As you begin thinking about your final project, review your body of work from our previous lessons. Look for patterns and themes and respond to the following questions.

◆ What works are you most proud of?
◆ What issues are you passionate about?
◆ What questions and subjects are you drawn to?
◆ What do you want to study further?

Used with permission from Fishman-Weaver and Clingan, Teaching Women's and Gender Studies. Copyright © 2023, Taylor and Francis, Inc.

Your final project should expand on a key idea, include an action component, and build on our course scholarship. You are the best person to define what success will mean for you in this project. Below is a planning chart to help organize your project.

Synthesis Project—Planning Chart			
	Key Idea	**Action**	**Scholarship**
Planning questions	◆ What is the focus of your project? How is that connected to Women's and Gender studies? ◆ How are you connected to this topic?	◆ How will this project make a difference in your community? ◆ Why will this project matter to you and your community?	◆ What specific resources will you cite in this project? ◆ How will you engage in research and knowledge production that affirms and honors our course lessons?
Lesson concepts	Justice (racial justice) Health disparities Food insecurity Representation Radical hope Inclusion Ending violence	Advocacy Solidarity Resistance	Lived experiences Feminisms Intersectionality History Policy Art Mental health

Impact

◆ What will success look like for you in this project?

◆ What do you want to celebrate?

◆ How will this project advance justice?

Used with permission from Fishman-Weaver and Clingan, Teaching Women's and Gender Studies. Copyright © 2023, Taylor and Francis, Inc.

Extension Resources for Concept 3

Black Is Beautiful—Resources on Natural Hair

Black women's hairstyles have long been policed and politicized. This chapter appendix includes two resources that celebrate the power of Black beauty and that advocate for resistance to Eurocentric and damaging beauty standards. The first is a TED Talk by Cheyenne Cochrane, and the second is the Oscar-winning short film, *Hair Love*. View these individually or as a whole class.

◆ What surprised you in these videos? What did you learn? What questions do you have?
◆ How do these videos relate to the WGST concepts we have learned?
◆ What connections can you draw between this conversation on natural hair and our book themes of resistance, representation, and radical hope?

The Policing of Women's Clothes at Work

 Thought Question

◆ What is your power outfit?

This is an outfit or article of clothing that makes you feel confident and ready for challenges.

I (Kathryn) asked three young women this question. One shared that her most meaningful article of clothing is a Mexican serape her mother gave her. It has her name embroidered on it. She told me when she wears the serape, she feels connected to her culture, her family, and "dreams of her ancestors." Another young woman said she loves how she feels at festivals and weddings when she gets to wear bright-colored saris and paint her arms with henna. Still a third said she has a glittery bright pink floor-length skirt she chooses whenever she's having a bad day. Like the first young person, this was also a gift from her mother. She says there is nothing else quite like it in her closet.

In the following activity, you will explore some of the policies and practices that have and continue to make it difficult for women and gender-expansive people to show up for work, particularly in the political sector. While these readings talk about the over policing of women's dress at work and victories won, there is still so much work to do to create professional cultures that not only accept but also celebrate bright colored serapes, pretty blue saris, glittery floor-length skirts, and any other garment that connects the wearer to their culture, family, heritage, and confidence.

Dress Codes in the U.S. Senate

In 1969, Representative Charlotte T. Reid (1913–2007) stirred up the Senate. The Republican representative had a history of being tough, but this reaction had nothing to do with legislation. Her congressional colleagues couldn't believe that she had worn pants to work (Linderman, 2017). Four years earlier, Reid had been one of the first members of Congress to visit war-torn South Vietnam. She paid her own way, riding helicopters into the war zone and reassuring American soldiers at the bases (The Office of the Historian, n.d.). But on that day, Senate politicians were shocked that she had broken a longstanding albeit unwritten dress code rule—that women don't wear pants on the Senate floor.

This unofficial rule persisted for decades until 1993 when Senators Barbara Mikulski (1936–), Nancy Kassebaum (1932–), and Carol Moseley-Braun (1947–) all showed up for work in pantsuits. The range of reactions ran from shock to gratitude. Senate doorkeepers could turn away anyone they deemed dressed inappropriately, and women for decades had to change clothes, sometimes more than once, before being approved by the doorkeeper. Because these rules about appropriate attire were unwritten, they were often inconsistent, so a woman wearing an outfit that had been approved by one doorkeeper might be made to change clothes by a different doorkeeper. The sergeant at arms is a Senate-elected position who serves as the chief law enforcement officer of the Senate and door keeper. This person is tasked with protecting the members of the Senate and maintaining security in all Senate buildings. In 1993, Martha Pope served as the sergeant at arms. She had been the first woman elected to this position (Cymrot, 2021), and she drafted a memo to announce to all door attendants that the dress code now included slacks for women (Linderman, 2017).

◆ What surprised you (or made you angry) in this reading?
◆ Was resisting the dress code a feminist act? Why or why not?
◆ Why do you think the dress code persisted for so long?
◆ What are the important firsts in this story? (Hint: There are several.)

Of course, the matter of what women and gender-expansive individuals wear to work, in the Senate and elsewhere, was not solved when Martha

Pope announced in 1993 that women could wear slacks on the Senate floor (Linderman, 2017). In 2020, Cori Bush (1976–), a U.S. representative from Missouri and a nurse, pastor, and activist, tweeted: "The reality of being a regular person going to Congress is that it's really expensive to get the business clothes I need for the Hill. So, I'm going thrift shopping tomorrow" (Bush, 2020). The problem that Bush faced in finding clothes that were considered acceptable for her job as a congresswoman is not confined to politics. This issue especially affects women and gender-expansive individuals. Women are much more likely to be criticized for their appearance at work than men. A 2017 study found that one in four women had been cautioned about their appearance at work. In contrast, according to the same study, fewer than one in ten men had been cautioned about their appearance (Pavey, 2017).

◆ How does the unequal emphasis on appearance affect the workplace?
◆ If you were in charge of a company, how would you create greater inclusion related to culture, dress, and gender?
◆ Are there ways you and your peers can impact change without being in charge of a company?

Be an Upstander

Term	Definition
Upstander	A person who intervenes to help victims of bullying or discrimination. An upstander uses their words or actions to support a person or cause.
Bystander	A person who observes bullying or discrimination but does not intervene or use their words or actions to help.

Throughout these lessons, you have learned about *advocacy, allyship*, and *solidarity*. In this activity, you will explore a related term—*upstander*. These terms all share a commitment to action, justice, and to standing up for others. Please note: the following activity addresses bullying and discrimination. This may bring up big feelings for you and your peers. If you are being bullied, feel unsafe at school (or elsewhere), or know of bullying happening in your community, please talk to a teacher or trusted adult.

In 2022, Amanda Gorman, the U.S. poet whose work you have read in several of our Women's and Gender Studies lessons, appeared on the PBS children's show *Sesame Street*. Watch the video *"Sesame Street*: Be an Upstander with Amanda Gorman." A link to the video is in the section appendix.

In this video, Amanda Gorman and Gabrielle teach Grover what an upstander is: "someone who uses their kind words or actions to help their friends or themselves when they are being treated unfairly or unkindly" and someone who treats everyone with "kindness, fairness, and respect." When you observe behavior that is unkind, unfair, or unsafe, you often have to make a choice between intervening and being an *upstander* or not intervening and being a *bystander*.

Unfortunately, there are many opportunities to choose between being an upstander and being a bystander. While some acts of bullying and discrimination are overt and violent, such as a fight in the hallway, more often they are quick, covert, or even quiet, such as a discriminatory comment or "joke" that passes quickly in a conversation. These include generalizations and biases about groups of people (particularly girls, women, people of color, and members of the LGBTQIA+ community). These smaller acts, also known as *microaggressions*, are hurtful and damaging. In the video segment, Amanda, Grover, and Gabrielle talk about how it is important to be an upstander when someone is being treated unfairly or unkindly for the color of their skin, shape of their eyes, language they speak, or religion. As a Women's and Gender Studies scholar, you have learned about racial justice, gender justice, LGBTQIA+ inclusion, representation, and resistance. How does being an upstander relate to these key themes?

Exit Questions

There are many ways to be an upstander. There are also often real consequences for choosing between being an upstander and being a bystander.

- ◆ What are some of the reasons it can be hard (or even unsafe) to be an upstander?
- ◆ What ideas do you have for intervening in these challenging situations?
- ◆ How can you use your creativity, your community, and your courage to respond to bullying and discrimination?
- ◆ Share an example of someone who was (or is) an upstander for gender justice or inclusion. (You might choose someone from your own experiences or someone from your WGST studies.)
- ◆ How can you be an upstander?

Fill in the Sentence Starter Below

I will be an upstander by _____

Bonus Extension Activity: In a small group with your peers, write and record a short skit similar to the *Sesame Street* video that could be used in younger grades to teach young scholars how to be an upstander.

Helpful Links

- ◆ GLSEN National Day of Silence: www.glsen.org/day-of-silence
- ◆ GLSEN Educator Resources: www.glsen.org/resources/educator-resources
- ◆ Video intro "Black is Beautiful" (Modeling and Photography): www.youtube.com/watch?v=LRAjdO_go5g
- ◆ "Black is Beautiful" and "Black Girl Magic" by Taylor Cassidy J.: www.youtube.com/watch?v=5LjuLhEh4yo
- ◆ Las Krudas "La Gorda": www.youtube.com/watch?v=Mlzf9BPHZYo
  - – Video Resources in Celebration of Black Hair Love
  - – *A Celebration of Natural Hair:* TED Talk by Cheyenne Cochrane: www.ted.com/talks/cheyenne_cochrane_a_celebration_of_natural_hair#t-823936
  - – *Hair Love:* Oscar-Winning short: www.youtube.com/watch?v=kN-w8V_Fkw28
- ◆ Amanda Gorman "Using Your Voice is a Political Choice": www.youtube.com/watch?v=zaZBgqfEa1E
- ◆ Amanda Gorman's "The Hill We Climb" performance: www.youtube.com/watch?v=LZ055ilIiN4&feature=emb_logo
- ◆ Amanda Gorman's "The Hill We Climb" transcript: https://thehill.com/homenews/news/535052-read-transcript-of-amanda-gormans-inaugural-poem?rl=1
- ◆ Ms. Opal Lee on Juneteenth (White House video): www.youtube.com/watch?v=mBVsjIjP_aI
- ◆ CBS video, "Civil Rights Pioneer Claudette Colvin Has Arrest Records Expunged": www.youtube.com/watch?v=XqOZ6OPaeps
- ◆ Frederick Douglass' descendants deliver his "Fourth of July" speech: www.npr.org/2020/07/03/884832594/video-frederick-douglass-descendants-read-his-fourth-of-july-speech
- ◆ Favianna Rodriguez, an interdisciplinary artist whose work explores the intersection of important justice issues: https://favianna.com/
- ◆ #ActuallyAutistic accounts to follow (several explore both disability and LGBTQIA+ identities and lived experiences): www.verywell-health.com/autism-instagram-accounts-5120708#:~:text=The%20%23ActuallyAutistic%20hashtag%20is%20one,people%20on%20the%20autism%20spectrum.
  - – You might start with autism_sketches: www.instagram.com/autism_sketches/
- ◆ Ms. Magazine "The Future of Disability Rights": https://msmagazine.com/2018/04/12/future-disability-rights-activism-female/
- ◆ Women's Disability Rights: A Timeline: http://whitneylewjames.com/disability-activism/

- Maggie Aderin-Pocock, PhD, space scientist & science communicator: https://dyslexia.yale.edu/story/maggie-aderin-pocock-ph-d/
- Amanda Gorman's interview with the *Today Show*: www.youtube.com/watch?v=OuOMApb1qBs
- Representation in U.S. currency (learn more about the six incredible women appearing on the U.S. quarters in 2022): www.cbsnews.com/news/here-are-the-women-who-will-be-appearing-on-quarters-in-2022/?fbclid=IwAR3FcPKK5nXyXNWCrlj_B0v4M3e23_VsEzD7zhSgTscumqJWrbaj5–6D7C4
- CNN article and video, "'Didn't See Ourselves Represented': This Figure Skating Pair is Ditching the Gender Norms Rooted in their Sport": www.cnn.com/videos/sports/2022/02/02/figure-skating-timothy-leduc-ashley-cain-gribble-winter-olympics-spt-intl-lon-orig-na.cnn
- *"Sesame Street*: Be and Upstander" with Amanda Gorman video: www.youtube.com/watch?v=vzpnitSjZA4

Notes

[1] The chapter appendix includes several links with helpful resources to organize your own Day of Silence.

[2] The chapter appendix includes two short video resources on the Black is Beautiful movement that you can share with scholars.

[3] Passinho is a dance that originated in the favelas and gained international acclaim following the 2016 Olympics. It has been cited as a dance form that has helped contribute to border crossing and bridge building between cultures.

[4] Unit 4 is rich with examples of artists, artivists, and feminist artists producing work for social change. While working through this lesson, you and your scholars may want to reference this unit.

[5] This statistical underrepresentation of girls and young women with autism diagnoses is due to several reasons, including gender bias in autism criteria and misdiagnosing girls with conditions such as attention-deficit hyperactivity disorder, obsessive-compulsive disorder, or anorexia (Agoratus and Alizo, 2016).

[6] You can find a few #ActuallyAutistic accounts to follow in the section appendix.

[7] To expunge means to erase or remove completely.

[8] Carmel, J. (2021). *The New York Times.*

[9] Matheus, who attends school in Campinas, SP, translated his interview from Portuguese to English. The original interview transcript was ten pages long.
[10] Source: Biskupik (2009)
[11] Justice Ginsburg frequently used this strategy to expand the court's interpretation of existing legislation such as the 14th Amendment or the Civil Rights Act.

Proseminar: Intersectionality

Foreword by Dr. Adrian Clifton, Advisory Editor

Dr. Adrian Chanel Clifton (she/her) is a proud alum of the University of Missouri-Columbia. While attending the university, she earned three degrees: a Bachelor of Science degree in elementary education, a master's degree in curriculum and instruction, and a doctoral degree in the area of learning, teaching, and curriculum. Dr. Clifton served as the first College of Education alum to teach abroad at a Mizzou Academy international partner school. It was an honor for both Dr. Clifton and her family to live in Brazil and experience their culture firsthand. Dr. Clifton has a background in poetry, hip hop, and fashion. She finds creative ways to connect her love of the arts to her students and the communities she serves.

At what intersections do you reside? What borders have you crossed? How do your identities (gender, sexual orientation, race, faith, ability, and socio-economic status) influence your everyday experiences? When has your race identity dictated the food you have access to? This is an example of the deep-rooted questions scholars will dig into in their study of *intersectionality*.

I first wrote about intersectionality in my dissertation in 2016. I used autoethnography to study the experiences of five Black women and girls, including myself, who were living at the intersections of race and poverty in Columbia, Missouri. In addition to radical hope, I discovered the power that

DOI: 10.4324/9781003289500-5

came from radical faith and radical relationships within radical community spaces. These ingredients were, and still are, vital for our survival.

Black women and girls are disproportionately affected by health disparities, including limited access to mental health services and early childcare options, as well as systemic inequities in educational practices and the welfare system (Love, 2020). School systems are burdened and Black girls are often subjected to harsh and unequal discipline policies that often push them out of school and into juvenile detention and adult prison institutions (Love, 2020; Morris, 2018). Yet it was at this same intersection where the Black girls in my study woke and rose for the day unapologetically. As a Black woman researcher, I was intrigued and curious about this "rose out of concrete"[1] mentality, even within myself.

My research led me to the fertilizer and water source for such roses. This radical community space was beyond concrete walls ordained in graffiti, past a bridge blaring with sirens, and just beyond yellow caution tape marking the third murder of the summer. There, in the Columbia Housing Projects, stood a brick home blooming with flowers kindrily known as Granny's House. Inside this space, Black girls read about their worth in biblical texts, studied for exams, ate dinner, and prayed before stepping out to cross the busy intersection leading home. This space was a lifeline for the girls and me. Granny's House is run by Pam and Dr. Ellis Ingram. "Granny Pam," as she is known to the whole city, shared stories and wisdom to help us navigate our lives and release and heal our traumas.

When I think about the complexities of intersectionality, I am reminded of Kat, who at the time of my study was a 16-year-old enthusiastic Black girl who wore her hair in a tight bun at the top of her head, religiously. Kat was a freshman at Hickman High School and the star player of the girls' basketball team. Colleges were already seeking her out. But many games, Kat played with a hungry stomach. During sophomore year, her mother was evicted from their home. She spent nights on my couch when I lived in an apartment in public housing.

In 2017, I got my first university position and moved into my first home. As a mother of four, Kat continued to come over to babysit for me. We held ice cream cones in our hands and made a toast on my behalf: "For movin on up in the world, Dr. A!" Kat exclaimed enthusiastically. I made her promise not to forget about "us small people" when she rose to become a famous philanthropist one day. Today Kat is making good on her promise. As a community activist in Kansas City, she is currently creating the blueprint for an ice cream shop in one of the toughest areas hit by crime. She will call it *Granny's House*. Kat and I shared radical faith within a radical relationship built at a radical community space.

As women our lives are constantly being affected by intersections. In this proseminar, scholars will study the works of Patricia Hill Collins and the Combahee Collective River Statement, and they will engage in further research on their own identities and experiences and those of the people they have studied. Like crossing guards on a busy intersection, Kathryn and Jill safely walk scholars through definitions, analytics, and research essential for students, educators, and activists to consider and think about critically. With a useful set of tools and references, scholars will be invited to create, celebrate, and connect to the world of justice work.

Teaching Notes

A proseminar is typically a course that is based on readings and dialogue around a specific topic. These courses are usually offered in graduate school but are also open to advanced undergraduate students. In the spirit of not having to wait to make a positive difference or to engage with challenging material, we (Kathryn and Jill) included a proseminar in this book that is tailored for middle school scholars. This proseminar will offer your class extended experiences in a foundational topic in Women's and Gender Studies—*intersectionality*.

You might teach this proseminar to your entire class/es or offer it as an enrichment seminar to a small group before or after school.

Our hope is that these activities expose scholars to deeper learning of a foundational concept for feminisms and justice work, exciting art, and activist projects.

The final proseminar project is an art making and research project in which scholars create two collages, one on their own identities and a second on the experiences and work of a key figure from our WGST Studies. Scholars will then engage in a compare and contrast where they draw connections between their stories (as a site of knowledge) and the stories of changemakers across a variety of fields. We recommend hosting a public gallery of the final pieces where scholars can share about their art making and the connections they made to their studies throughout the earlier lessons and their proseminar content.

In her poem "Quilting the Black-Eyed Pea (We're Going to Mars)," U.S. poet and activist Nikki Giovanni (2010) states: "The trip to Mars can only be understood through Black Americans" (line 73–74).[2] Sit with that idea for a moment.

◆ What evidence might support such a claim?
◆ What does this idea have to do with justice?
◆ On whose wisdom do we draw as we journey forward?

In this proseminar, you will learn more about intersectionality. While you have encountered this term throughout our studies, the following activities give you an opportunity to go deeper with your learning about this foundational concept.

INTERSECTIONALITY A framework for understanding how multiple identities and *systems of oppressions* intersect to create specific experiences and conditions within systems.		
KEY POINT 1—Our experiences happen within systems of advantage (power and privilege) and disadvantage (discrimination and oppression).	KEY POINT 2— Experiences and identities are overlapping.	KEY POINT 3— Stories are sites of knowledge.
The ways institutions, structures, and norms reinforce discrimination, including, but not limited to, sexism, racism, classism, heterosexism, ableism, and ageism, is called the *system of oppression* (or *matrix of domination*). Systems of oppression are socially and historically specific and connected to power. Patricia Hill Collins is a leading thought leader in this area.	An intersectional approach centers the experiences and "voices of those experiencing overlapping, concurrent forms of oppression in order to understand outsider the depths of the inequalities and the relationships among them in any given context" (UN Women, 2020, para 5).	Intersectional approaches believe that first-person experiences and stories, particularly of individuals from historically marginalized and multiply marginalized backgrounds, are important sites for knowledge.

Outsider Within—Patricia Hill Collins

Dr. Patricia Hill Collins (1948–) is an American social theorist whose work focuses on race, class, gender, and sexuality. While we have all had outsider experiences, Collins' (1986) *outsider within* standpoint refers to the specific racialized and gendered context that Black women navigate in society. This context matters. Black feminisms center the specific and collective voices and experiences of Black women. Dr. Collins' book *Black Feminist Thought: Knowledge, Consciousness, and the Politics of Empowerment* (first published in 1990) is a leading work on systems of oppression and the intersection of social, racial, and gender justice.

Black Feminist Thought—*The Combahee River Collective Statement*

Formed in 1974, The Combahee River Collective aimed to create a space and agenda where the voices and experiences of Black women lesbians were included and centered in the work for justice. In a time in U.S. history known for civil rights and women's rights work (1960–1970s), this particular group was often excluded from justice movements. Mainstream feminism often left out people of color, and the national liberation movements for racial justice often excluded women. The Combahee River Collective Statement published in 1977 became a seminal piece in its statement of feminist history in the United States. It is considered critical early literature on Black feminism, intersectionality, and identity politics.

On Whose Shoulders?

The name *Combahee River* refers to a Union Army raid led by Harriet Tubman. Harriet Tubman, known as the "Moses of her people," is considered the first African American woman to serve in the military. A formerly enslaved person herself, Tubman dedicated her life to helping enslaved people gain their freedom. During the Combahee River raid, which Tubman helped lead, 750 enslaved people in South Carolina were liberated. In addition to honoring Harriet Tubman, feminists in the Combahee River Collective say the name serves as a reminder that liberation requires political action (Taylor, 2020).

Jigsaw Analysis—In this activity, scholars will work in teams of three or six to analyze excerpts from the Combahee River Collective Statement (1977), connecting them to key concepts from Dr. Patricia Hill Collins' *Outsider Within* (*1986)* article and their own experiences.

Jigsaw Steps

First—Using the reflective questions below, work independently to analyze one of the excerpts below.

Next—In groups, share your responses to the questions and reactions to each excerpt.

Finally—Respond to this prompt: How are systems of oppression present in your community, and what are some ways you and your peers can disrupt these patterns of injustice?

Excerpt	Key Concept	Text from *Combahee River Collective Statement* (2015)
Primary Source Jigsaw Analysis—Black Feminisms, United States (1970–1980s) Excerpt from the *Combahee River Collective Statement* (1977) republished in *This Bridge Called My Back: Writings by Radical Women of Color* (2015)		
A	Our experiences happen within systems of advantage (power and privilege) and disadvantage (discrimination and oppression).	The most general statement of our politics at the present time would be that we are actively committed to struggling against racial, sexual, heterosexual, and class oppression and see as our particular task the development of integrated analysis and practice based upon the fact that the major systems of oppression are interlocking. The synthesis of these oppressions creates the conditions of our lives. As Black women we see Black feminism as the logical political movement to combat the manifold and simultaneous oppressions that all women of color face (p. 210).
B	Experiences and identities are overlapping.	A political contribution which we feel we have already made is the expansion of the feminist principle that the personal is political. In our consciousness-raising sessions, for example, we have in many ways gone beyond white women's revelations because we are dealing with the implications of race and class as well as sex (p. 213).
C	Stories are sites of knowledge.	Above all else, our politics initially sprang from the shared belief that Black women are inherently valuable, that our liberation is a necessity not as an adjunct to somebody else's but because of our need as human persons for autonomy. This may seem so obvious as to sound simplistic, but it is apparent that no other ostensibly progressive movement has ever considered our specific oppression as a priority or worked seriously for the ending of that oppression (p. 212).

Concepts from P.H. Collins, Outsider Within *(1986)*

Reflective Questions

- Summarize your excerpt in your own words. What is the key message?
- Connect this excerpt to one of the key terms of vocabulary from our WGST lessons.
- Connect this excerpt to a specific historical event or person's work.
- Connect this excerpt to your own lives and community. How does this message relate to something you have experienced or witnessed in your community or the news?
- What are your reactions to this statement? What do you agree with? What would you challenge? Are there any points you would like to qualify with more information?

Exit Question: How are systems of oppression present in your community, and what are some ways you and your peers can disrupt these patterns of injustice?

Proseminar Project—Identity Collages, Research, and Radical Hope

Name_____ Date_____

Guiding Questions
◆ What can you learn from exploring a more complete personal history?
◆ How can an intersectional understanding support justice work?

Background: This proseminar project has three parts.

◆ Part I—Identity Collage (on you!)
◆ Part II—Research Collage (on key figure)
◆ Part III—Radical Hope Reflection

Part I—Identity Collage

Building on our proseminar activities, this project celebrates your experiences, cultures, identities, and backgrounds as important sites for knowledge. Through this activity, you will have the opportunity to reflect on your multiple identities, strengths, and talents and the way your story can inspire you to engage in justice work.

Directions

◆ Create a list of your identities.
  Consider: race, ethnicity, national origin, age, gender, faith or religious affiliation, home language, (dis)ability, and others.
◆ Create a list of the different social groups to which you belong.
  Consider: family, friends/peers, sports and activities, faith communities, neighborhoods, and others.
◆ Consider other key identity markers that represent your strengths and make you—you.
  Consider: personal motto, favorite color, strengths/talents, passions, favorite place, favorite food, hobbies, etc.
◆ Gather photographs, artifacts, and magazine or newspaper clippings that illustrate key items from each of the three categories.
◆ Get creative! Collage your materials into a self-portrait. You may interpret "self-portrait" as literally or abstractly as you like.

Reflection Questions

◆ What surprised you in creating your identity collage? Reread the earlier definition of *intersectionality*. How do your identities work in concert or conflict with each other?

Used with permission from Fishman-Weaver and Clingan, Teaching Women's and Gender Studies. Copyright © 2023, Taylor and Francis, Inc.

◆ What role does power play in your personal identities and experiences?
◆ What identities are most important to you? What makes these identities important?
◆ Are there identities that you seldom think about? Why do you think that is?
◆ What social groups are most important to you? What makes those groups important?
◆ Where can you find examples of representation, resistance, or radical hope in your "identity collage"?

Part II—Research Collage

Throughout these lessons, you have met scholars, psychologists, authors, activists, and teachers engaged in powerful justice work. Select **one** of the key figures introduced in these lessons and answer the questions below. Go beyond our lessons and learn through additional research!

Sojourner Truth	**bell hooks**	**Amanda Gorman**
Chimamanda Adichie	**Audre Lorde**	**Malala Yousafzai**
Kamala Harris	**Shamsia Hassani**	**Opal Lee**

◆ Create a list of their identities.
  Consider: race, ethnicity, national origin, age, gender, faith or religious affiliation, home language, (dis)ability, and others.
◆ Create a list of the different social groups to which they belong(ed).
  Consider: family, friends/peers, sports and activities, faith communities, neighborhoods, and others.
◆ Consider other key identity markers that represent their strengths and works.
  What can you learn about them personally and professionally?
◆ Gather photographs, artifacts, and magazine or newspaper clippings that illustrate key items from each of the three categories listed.
◆ Get creative! Collage your materials into a portrait. As discussed earlier, you may interpret "portrait" as literally or abstractly as you like.

Reflective Questions

◆ What surprised you in creating this new identity collage? Read the definition of intersectionality above. How do the identities and experiences in this collage work in concert or conflict with each other?
◆ What role does or did power and agency play in the work, identities, and experiences of your key figure?
◆ What identities were easiest to find information about? Which identities were hardest to find information about? Why do you think that is?

Used with permission from Fishman-Weaver and Clingan, Teaching Women's and Gender Studies. Copyright © 2023, Taylor and Francis, Inc.

- ◆ What aspects of your key figure's identity, experiences, and work did you choose to celebrate and why?
- ◆ Where can you find examples of representation, resistance, or radical hope in your "research collage"?

Part III—Radical Hope Reflection, Research, and Art Statement

As the final piece of your proseminar project, write a research and artist statement on these two collages. You may present your statement as a paper, an audio recording, or poster.

> Prompt: Compare and contrast your two identity collages. What do you notice that makes you proud? What questions do you still have about identity and intersectionality? In making your collages, what aspects did you choose to celebrate? What are your takeaways from your research, and how will you use these ideas in your life and community?

A final thought: Centering radical hope does not ignore or erase discriminatory and problematic practices—conversely, focusing on hope calls these practices out plainly and says that with intentionally we can (and must) do better (Fishman-Weaver, 2017).

Used with permission from Fishman-Weaver and Clingan, Teaching Women's and Gender Studies. Copyright © 2023, Taylor and Francis, Inc.

Helpful Links

Nikki Giovanni, "Quilting the Black-Eyed Pea (We're going to Mars)": www.youtube.com/watch?v=cMKSSlaqTLE

Notes

[1] This is a reference to "The Rose That Grew Out of Concrete," a poem by Tupac Shakur about thriving in places that are inhospitable to growth.

[2] You can find a link to Giovanni performing this poem in the section appendix.

Epilogue

By Advisory Editor Dr. Dena Lane-Bonds

Dr. Dena Lane-Bonds (she/her) is a postdoctoral research scholar for the Initiative for Race Research and Justice in the Department of Teaching and Learning at Vanderbilt University. She received her PhD in educational leadership and policy analysis from the University of Missouri, where she studied the experiences of graduate students navigating homelessness and housing insecurity. In higher education, her research and efforts have been centered on cultivating equitable and inclusive teaching, learning, and working environments. Her recent works have explored the pathways to leadership for Black women.

In my research, I gravitate towards narrative methodologies. In doing so, I am unequivocally aware of whose stories are documented, overlooked, and disseminated over time. Therefore, in my work and practice, I strive to decenter the dominant discourse, expose privilege and other oppressive systems, and deconstruct deficit views of individuals from marginalized communities. In the same vein, the book you have just read, *Teaching Women's and Gender Studies*, is filled with authentic stories that highlight the experiences of women and their fruitful contributions to their communities, physical environments, and their students.

In light of the growing focus on controlling whose voices are represented in the K-12 curriculum, this timely text has highlighted the importance of

DOI: 10.4324/9781003289500-6

representing diverse voices and experiences, and the victories of women through historical and current events. Many of the conversations on feminism occur in higher education. Kathryn Fishman-Weaver and Jill Clingan made groundbreaking efforts by introducing and making widely accessible culturally relevant feminist perspectives in the K-12 classroom. Centering issues of race, gender, place, and equity and documenting challenges across the Global North and South, you and your scholars have explored meaningful ways that women have disrupted troubling trends within their social, political, and environmental landscapes.

This text revealed the strong need for teachers to gain a deeper understanding of the intersections of race, gender, and its influence on curriculum and classroom interactions. These lessons gave an account of how women have been overlooked and disregarded through time and how through such challenges, they have overcome and disrupted racist and sexist acts and advanced justice. The authors wove together compelling historical accounts that confront racism, gendered norms, and hierarchies that create a hostile environment for women academically, politically, and socially.

In this book, educators learn feminist, womanist, mujerista, and Indigenous ways of understanding, including our connection to one another. As you carry these lessons forward, this book encourages educators to (1) acknowledge, teach, and share complete histories and counterstories; (2) uphold asset-based practices and illuminate gendered and racial dynamics; and (3) and enact change within your classrooms and communities. The list of reflection questions and guided action plans can help continue this important conversation and guide your classroom to be a space that is inclusive, welcomes critical conversation, and initiates change.

Overall, Kathryn Fishman-Weaver and Jill Clingan have offered new perspectives on how the experiences of women have led to transformational outcomes. This text is an excellent resource for all educators and can serve as an exceptional model for a multifaceted and inclusive perspective on feminism. Most important, *Teaching Women's and Gender Studies* advocates for educators to understand that "love is a combination of care, commitment, knowledge, responsibility, respect and trust " (hooks, 2002, p. 131) to self, others, and to the world we all call home.

Glossary

Term	Definition	Unit
Ableism	Discrimination against the disability community, including overt discrimination, erasing disabilities, casting disabilities as inherent deficits, and not creating accessible solutions or environments where all can thrive.	5
Abolition	The ending of a practice, system, or institution often in reference to institutional racism or the systematic denial of human rights such as human enslavement.	5
Advocacy	The act of supporting and working toward a specific cause, which can include organizing, educating, lobbying, training, and mobilizing.	2
Affective development	The capacity to recognize, experience, and express a broad range of emotions and the ability to respond well to the emotions and emotional cues of others. Affective development is a process that happens over time as people learn more about their emotional state, emotional regulation, and strategies to navigate our social world.	3
American Sign Language (ASL)	The sign language most used in the United States deaf community. It is a language composed of hand motions, body movements, and facial expressions.	4
Artivism	A combination of art and activism, whereby artists address injustice, inequities, and other social challenges through creative expression. Artivists aim to increase awareness of social issues and reimagine and reclaim new possibilities through their work. Artivists may use a variety of media, including slam poetry, music, dance, mural, performance art, large-scale installations, and graphic design.	5

Binary	Consisting of only two parts (related: binary thinking or believing there are only two parts).	1
Bystander	A person who observes bullying or discrimination but does not intervene or use their words or actions to help.	6
Cisgender	People whose gender aligns with the sex they were assigned at birth. For example, if a baby was assigned male at birth and identifies as a boy/man, he would be considered cisgender (or cis).	1
Colonization	To violently establish control over the Indigenous people of an area. This control is intended to benefit those coming to the land and colonizing, even at the great harm of those who have previously cared for and called the land home. In addition to physical harm, Indigenous traditions and culture are often devalued or destroyed during colonization.	1
Disability	In terms of legislative definitions, the Americans with Disabilities Act (ADA) and the Individuals with Disabilities Act (IDEA) shape most of the policy around disability in the United States. Disability is largely contextualized by the personal—and social—meanings that individuals ascribe to this identity. This means that families, teachers, and people with disabilities all have a lot of power to reconstruct how we understand disability. As one part of a child's identity, disability can contribute to specific strengths and challenges. Having a disability is both complex and limited in what it can (and can't) tell us. Further, disability is malleable; how it presents, the meanings we ascribe to it, and the significance it carries can all change over the course of an individual's life (Fishman-Weaver, 2019)	5

Disability rights	A global social movement to expand access, rights, and opportunities to members of the disability community.	5
Equality	Having the same status, rights, and opportunities.	1
Equity	Fairness and justice; equity is different from equality (see equality) in that it recognizes that different people have different experiences, opportunities, access, and needs. Because of this, equity work requires systematic change to remove barriers, adjust imbalances, and create more just solutions and systems.	1
Eurocentrism	Excluding or omitting the multiple global perspectives, experiences, cultures, and histories that make our world and casting European culture and history as the norm.	3
Feminism	An affirmation of humanity that seeks freedom from oppression and commits to the full access of social, health, economic, and political rights and opportunities for all people. (See also the definitions and discussion of Black feminisms, transnational and global feminisms, queer theory, liberal feminisms, and radical feminisms.)	1
Feminist Art Movement	An expansive multi-media arts movement that sought to (1) provide greater gender representation in art, (2) correct for and expose the erasure of women's stories and full identities, (3) and resist the reproduction of gender stereotypes in art (Rise Art, 2021).	4
Gender	Socially constructed and culturally specific roles, behaviors, and identities of being feminine, masculine, or a combination of traits.	1
Gender-expansive	An umbrella term for people whose gender expression and identity are beyond or outside a specific gender identity, category, or label. As an umbrella term, *gender-expansive* encompasses	1

	many different identities. Some gender-expansive people use this term when referencing their gender identity and some prefer other related terms. For example,	
	<ul><li>Some gender-expansive people identify with a spectrum of genders and may use the term *nonbinary*.</li><li>Some gender-expansive people identify primarily with a single gender and may use the term *transgender*,</li><li>and still other gender-expansive people may identify without a gender and use the term *agender*.</li></ul>As with all identity labels, it is important to honor the terms and language individual's identify with while also respecting that language can change over time.	
Gender parity	The equal participation and representation of genders within an organization, position, or population. Achieving gender parity in the highest levels of government would mean that as many women serve in these highest offices as do men.	5
Global feminisms	The intentional study of feminisms from around the world. This study is grounded in an ethics of inclusion. Global feminisms explore local feminisms and justice movements, transnational approaches (or those that move beyond geographical boundaries), and global trends such as those in the United Nations' Sustainable Development Goals. The Vanderbilt Global Feminisms Collective (n.d.) writes that Global feminisms scholars are engaged in the study of boundaries associated with sex, gender, sexuality, class, race, ability, ethnicity, geography, identity, and membership—using both theoretical and empirical lenses. They are attentive to silence and marginalization,	1

	to citizenship politics (including migration, refugees, rights, and participation), to political economy (formal and informal), to society and culture, and to the environment (understood as the places where we live, work, play, and pray). (para 3)	
Identity-first language	In more recent years, some members of the disability community have advocated for identity-first language, for example, *autistic person*. This choice can center and celebrate a person's disability identity and their personhood. As with all identities, if you are unsure how a person would like to be referenced, ask. If you can't access, err on the side of respect, dignity, and inclusion.	5
Intersectionality	A framework for understanding how multiple identities and *systems of oppressions* intersect to create specific experiences and conditions within systems. These experiences include systems of advantage (power and privilege) and disadvantage (discrimination and oppression). For example, these may include the compounding effects of racism and sexism, or racism and heterosexism, or racism, sexism, and heterosexism. This framework centers the experiences and "voices of those experiencing overlapping, concurrent forms of oppression in order to understand outside the depths of the inequalities and the relationships among them in any given context" (UN Women, 2020, para 5). Recognizing the first-person experiences and stories of individuals from historically marginalized and multiply marginalized backgrounds as important sites for knowledge is inherent to intersectional approaches.	1
Intersex	A general term used for a variety of situations in which a person's reproductive anatomy doesn't fit the binary definitions of "female" or "male."	1

Juneteenth	Considered the longest standing African American holiday and is often celebrated with festivals, food, music, and heritage. The history of this important day begins in 1863 with Abraham Lincoln's Emancipation Proclamation declaring that all enslaved people be set free. Two and a half years later on "Juneteenth" (June 19, 1865), federal troops stormed Galveston, Texas, to enforce the emancipation proclamation. More than 250,000 people were freed as a result of these actions. Galveston, Texas, was considered to be the last place in the United States not observing Lincoln's declaration. Six months after Juneteenth, the 13th Amendment was passed which constitutionally outlawed human enslavement.	6
Liberal feminisms	A framework that operates *within* systems to improve them. Cornerstones of this framework include working toward equal opportunity, access, individual rights, liberty, and legislative equity (Fishman-Weaver, 2017). Establishing better sexual harassment or equal opportunity hiring practices are examples of initiatives that liberal feminists might advocate for.	2
Misgender	To refer to someone by a name, pronoun, or other identifier that is inconsistent with their gender or gender identity.	5
Mural	A painting or work of art made directly on a wall or building.	4
Neurodiversity	The belief that differences and disabilities represent necessary and important variance in the human genome. Neurodiversity offers a strengths-based approach to disability and those who live, learn, perceive, and think differently.	5
Patriarchy	A system of government, society, or family in which men hold power and women are systematically excluded from power. Feminist movements seek to dismantle patriarchal systems and establish more equitable systems.	2

People-first language	Language that puts the person before the disability, for example, *a person with autism*. People-first language emerged from disability rights work in the 1990s and purposefully pushed against outdated and deficit terms for talking about disability such as handicapped. People-first language is generally considered the most respectful option unless you know that an individual or community prefers a different convention, such as identity-first language (see identity-first language).	5
Personal pronoun	A word that can be used to refer to someone in place of their name that indicates their gender identity. ◆ Examples include she/ella/him/they/zir.	5
Policy	A norm, rule, law, or course of action required by an organization, government, business, group, or individual. The four types of policies include public policy, organizational policy, functional policy, and specific policy.	6
Political	Although often related to government work, in the context of our studies, *political* refers to the way an idea or an ideal translates to direct action.	3
Queer theory	A critical framework that challenges power dynamics related to gender and sexuality. Queer theory rejects essentialist (or pre-determined) definitions and binary thinking. Rather than assuming that categories of gender, sex, and sexuality are natural and fixed, queer theorists seek a more nuanced understanding of gender as dynamic and negotiated. This framework celebrates a full spectrum of identities. Queer theory frameworks are used in literary criticism, political criticism, sociology studies, and more layered accounts of history. (See especially Gloria Anzaldúa, Adrienne Rich, Judith Butler, and Eve Kosofsky Sedgwick.)	2

Radical feminisms	A framework that operates *beyond* systems to construct new structures and possibilities. Radical feminists believe that our systems are so deeply rooted in inequity and oppression that must be fundamentally deconstructed, reimagined, and built anew. A famous radical feminist text is Audre Lorde's essay "The Master's Tools Will Never Dismantle the Master's House" (2015).	2
Reparations	To make right or repair; the making of amends for a wrong one has done by resources or other tangible support to those who have been wronged.	6
Scholarship	The academic study of and/or commitment to learning at a high level.	1
Sex	A label (female or male) assigned at birth based on reproductive anatomy, chromosomes, and biology.	1
Social construct	An idea that has been created, accepted, and reinforced across a cultural group (e.g. gender and race).	1
Social emotional learning (SEL)	Teaching and learning that is focused on health, connection, and care. SEL includes learning about emotions, identities, healthy relationships, attitudes and mindsets, empathy, and decision making.	3
Street art	Art that is created on public spaces including buildings, walls, and trains.	4
Strengths-based approaches	Also known as *asset-based approaches*, these represent a commitment to focus on strengths, assets, talents, and genius. Key questions include: What is going well? What are my or my community's strengths? ◆ The opposite of strengths-based approaches are *deficit-based approaches*.	3

Transgender	People whose gender does not align with the sex they were assigned at birth. For example, if a baby was assigned male at birth and later identifies as a girl/woman, she may be transgender (or trans).	1
Transnational feminisms	A methodology that seeks global action and understanding. It strives to move beyond individual nations or nation-states to engage in a more collective production of knowledge.	1
Universal design	Designing or reimagining a space, building, or organization to be as accessible and inclusive as possible. Universal design does not only benefit people with disabilities but can also improve the user experience for all. For example, consider how ramps help caregivers pushing strollers and how automatic doors help anyone carrying a heavy load.	5
United Nations' Sustainable Development Goals (SDG)	The United Nations' Sustainable Development plan outlines 17 goals called the SDGs for peace, prosperity, and wellbeing for humanity and the planet we share. ◆ SDG 1—No poverty ◆ SDG 2—Zero Hunger ◆ SDG 3—Good Health and Wellbeing ◆ SDG 4—Quality Education ◆ SDG 5—Gender Equality ◆ SDG 6—Clean Water and Sanitation ◆ SDG 7—Affordable and Clean Energy ◆ SDG 8—Decent Work and Economic Growth ◆ SDG 9—Industry, Innovation, and Infrastructure ◆ SDG 10—Reduced Inequalities ◆ SDG 11—Sustainable Cities and Communities ◆ SDG 12—Responsible Consumption and Production ◆ SDG 13—Climate Action ◆ SDG 14—Life Below Water ◆ SDG 15—Life on Land ◆ SDG 16—Peace, Justice, and Strong Institutions ◆ SDG 17—Partnerships for the Goals	1

| Upstander | A person who intervenes to help victims of bullying or discrimination. An upstander uses their words or actions to support a person or cause. | 6 |
| Women's and Gender Studies (WGST) | An interdisciplinary study of the ways gender is constructed and how it affects our lived experiences and opportunities; a commitment to work toward greater justice and equity; and the intentional centering of stories, histories, and contributions of women, girls that are too often missing from curricula and media. | 1 |

References

1981 Audre Lorde, "the Uses of Anger: Women Responding to Racism." (2012, August 12). *Blackpast*. Retrieved October 20, 2021, from www.blackpast.org/african-american-history/speeches-african-american-history/1981-audre-lorde-uses-anger-women-responding-racism/

Adichie, C. N. (2014). *We Should All Be Feminists*. Vintage.

Afrobubblegum. (n.d.). *Afrobubblegum*. Retrieved September 23, 2021, from www.afrobubblegum.com

Agoratus, L., & Alizo, M. (2016, October 1). How Autism Manifests Differently in Girls: What Families Need to Know. *Autism Spectrum News*. Retrieved March 21, 2022, from https://autismspectrumnews.org/how-autism-manifests-differently-in-girls-what-families-need-to-know/

American Art Therapy Association. (2017). *American Art Therapy Association*. Retrieved March 19, 2022, from www.arttherapy.org/upload/2017_DefinitionofProfession.pdf

Amnesty International. (2021, October 11). *Its Intersex Awareness Day: Here Are 5 Myths We Need to Shatter*. www.amnesty.org/en/latest/news/2018/10/its-intersex-awareness-day-here-are-5-myths-we-need-to-shatter/

Amobi, F. (2021, December 13). Embracing an Asset-Based Model of Neurodiversity: Challenges and Academic Supports. *OSU Center for Teaching and Learning*. https://blogs.oregonstate.edu/osuteaching/2021/12/13/embracing-an-asset-based-model-of-neurodiversity-challenges-and-academic-supports/

APA Dictionary of Psychology. (n.d.). American Psychological Association. Retrieved January 9, 2022, from https://dictionary.apa.org/empathy

Archwy, A. (2021, April 12). Krudas Cubensi Wants the Freedom of Cuba, of All Countries, of All Bodies. *Archyworldys*. Retrieved January 3, 2022, from www.archyworldys.com/krudas-cubensi-wants-the-freedom-of-cuba-of-all-countries-of-all-bodies/

Armstead, R. (2007, Spring). "Growing the Size of the Black Woman": Feminist Activism in Havana Hip Hop. *NWSA Journal, 19*(1), 106–117. www.jstor.org/stable/4317233

The Art Story. (n.d.). *Feminist Art Movement Overview*. Retrieved October 23, 2021, from www.theartstory.org/movement/feminist-art/

Artsy. (n.d.). *Christine Sun Kim: 15 Artworks, Bio & Shows on Artsy*. Retrieved October 20, 2021, from www.artsy.net/artist/christine-sun-kim

Associated Press. (2021). Opal Lee's Juneteenth Dream Came True, But She Isn't Done. *U.S. News.* www.usnews.com/news/us/articles/2021-10-07/opal-lees-juneteenth-dream-came-true-but-she-isnt-done

Azzi, A. (2022, January 8). Non-Binary Figure Skater Timothy LeDuc Wins U.S. Pairs' Title with Cain-Gribble. *NBC Sports.* Retrieved March 1, 2022, from https://onherturf.nbcsports.com/2022/01/08/non-binary-figure-skater-timothy-leduc-ashley-cain-gribble-national-title/

Begnaud, D., & Reardon, S. (2021, December 16). Claudette Colvin, Arrested for Not Giving Up Her Seat for a White Woman in 1955, Has Record Expunged: "My Name Was Cleared: I'm No Longer a Juvenile Delinquent at 82." *CBS News.* www.cbsnews.com/news/claudette-colvin-record-expunged/

Bishop, R. S. (1990). Mirrors, Windows, and Sliding Glass Doors. *Perspectives,* 6(3), ix–xi.

Biskupik, J. (2009, May 5). Ginsburg: Court Needs Another Woman: USATODAY. com. *USA Today.* Retrieved March 2, 2022, from https://usatoday30.usatoday.com/news/washington/judicial/2009-05-05-ruthginsburg_N.htm

Bruna, D. (1975). *Lisa and Lynn.* Two Continents.

Budryk, Z. (2019, October 10). Pennsylvania Candidate Would Be First Autistic Woman Elected to a State Legislature. *The Hill.* https://thehill.com/homenews/state-watch/465169-pennsylvania-candidate-would-be-first-autistic-woman-elected-to-a-state?rl=1

Bush, Cori. [@CoriBush]. (2020, November 10). *The Reality of Being a Regular Person Going to Congress Is That It's Really Expensive to Get the Business Clothes* [Tweet]. Twitter. https://twitter.com/coribush/status/1326345538871156738

Butler, J. (1999). *Gender Trouble: Feminism and the Subversion of Identity* (2nd ed.). Routledge.

Carmel, J. (2021, June 18). Who Is Opal Lee? Her Campaign to Make Juneteenth a Holiday. *The New York Times.* www.nytimes.com/2020/06/18/style/opal-lee-juneteenth.html

Choi, C. (2020, October 21). Street Art Activism: What White People Call Vandalism. *Harvard Political Review.* https://harvardpolitics.com/street-art-activism/

CNN—bell hooks. (2000, February 17). *CNN.* Retrieved March 20, 2022, from http://edition.cnn.com/chat/transcripts/2000/2/hooks/index.html

Collins, P. H. (1986). Learning from the Outsider Within: The Sociological Significance of Black Feminist Thought. *Social Problems,* 33(6), S14–S32. https://doi.org/10.2307/800672

Combahee River Collective. (2015). A Black Feminist Statement. In C. Moraga & G. Anzaldúa (Eds.), *This Bridge Called My Back: Writings by Radical Women of Color* (4th ed., pp. 210–218). State University of New York Press.

Cymrot, S. (2021, August 6). *The Life's Work of Martha S. Pope*. HillRag. https://www.hillrag.com/2021/08/06/the-lifes-work-of-martha-s-pope/

Ellis-Petersen, H. (2019, April 8). "I am Not Here to Entertain": Meet Thailand's First Transgender MP. *The Guardian*. Retrieved March 1, 2022, from www.theguardian.com/world/2019/apr/06/i-am-not-here-to-entertain-meet-thailands-first-transgender-mp

Emma Amos. (n.d.) The Women's Studio: Striving for Parity. https://thewomensstudio.net/2018/04/30/emma-amos/

Encyclopedia Britannica. (2020). First Women to Lead Their Countries. *Britannica Presents 100 Women Trailblazers*. Retrieved March 20, 2022, from www.britannica.com/explore/100women/the-women/first-woman-to-lead-their-country

Enos, T. (2018, September 13). 8 Things You Should Know about Two Spirit People. *Indian Country Today*. https://indiancountrytoday.com/archive/8-misconceptions-things-know-two-spirit-people

Fishman-Weaver, K. (2017). A Call to Praxis: Using Gendered Organizational Theory to Center Radical Hope in Schools. *Journal of Organizational Theory in Education*, 2(1), 1–14.

Fishman-Weaver, K. (2018). *Wholehearted Teaching of Gifted Young Women*. Prufrock Press.

Fishman-Weaver, K. (2019). *When Your Child Learns Differently: A Family Approach for Navigating Special Education Services with Love and High Expectations* (1st ed.). Routledge.

Fishman-Weaver, K., & Walter, S. (2022). *Connected Classrooms: A Person-Centered Approach to Online, Blended, and In-Person Learning*. Solution Tree.

Ford, D. (2020, February 7). Social-Emotional Learning for Black Students Is Ineffective When It Is Culture-Blind. *Diverse: Issues in Higher Education*. www.diverseeducation.com/demographics/african-american/article/15106240/social-emotional-learning-for-black-students-is-ineffective-when-it-is-culture-blind

Free & Equal United Nations for LGBTI Equality. (n.d.). *Violence against Lesbian, Gay, Bisexual or Transgender People*. https://www.unfe.org/wp-content/uploads/2018/10/Violence-English.pdf

Gay, G. (2002). Preparing for Culturally Responsive Teaching. *Journal of Teacher Education*, 53(2), 106–116.

Gettleman, J. (2018, February 17). The Peculiar Position of India's Third Gender. *The New York Times*. www.nytimes.com/2018/02/17/style/india-third-gender-hijras-transgender.html

Giovanni, N. (2010). *Quilting the Black-Eyed Pea: Poems and Not Quite Poems* (Reprint ed.). William Morrow.

Global Feminisms Collaborative. (n.d.). Global Feminisms Collaborative: GFC Home. *Vanderbilt College of Arts and Science.* https://as.vanderbilt.edu/archived/gfc/www.vanderbilt.edu/gfc/

Holcomb, B. (2021). Ladyboys (Kathoeys) | Encyclopedia.com. *Encyclopedia. Com.* www.encyclopedia.com/social-sciences/encyclopedias-almanacs-transcripts-and-maps/ladyboys-kathoeys

hooks, b. (2002). *Communion: The Female Search for Love (Love Song to the Nation, 2).* William Morrow Paperbacks.

hooks, b. (2014). *Feminist Theory: From Margin to Center* (3rd ed.). Routledge.

hooks, b. (2020). *Feminism Is for Everybody: Passionate Politics* South End Press.

HRC Staff. (2020, November 23). Two Spirit and LGBTQ+ Identities: Today and Centuries Ago. *HRC.* www.hrc.org/news/two-spirit-and-lgbtq-idenitites-today-and-centuries-ago

Ibrahim, S. (2021, January 11). Stanford Community Reflects on Passing of Black Feminist Scholar Bell Hooks '73. *The Stanford Daily.* https://stanford daily.com/2021/12/22/stanford-community-reflects-on-passing-of-black-feminist-scholar-bell-hooks-73/

Illich, L., & Alter Smith, M. (2018, January). *Teach Living Poets.* https://teachliving poets.com

Indian Health Service. (n.d.). *Two-Spirit | Health Resources.* Indian Health Service The Federal.

Johari, A. (2014, April 17). Hijra, Kothi, Aravani: A Quick Guide to Transgender Terminology. *Scroll. In.* Retrieved March 23, 2022, from https://scroll.in/article/662023/hijra-kothi-aravani-a-quick-guide-to-transgender-terminology

Kahiu, W. (2017). Fun, Fierce and Fantastical African Art. *TED Talks.* Retrieved September 24, 2021, from www.ted.com/talks/wanuri_kahiu_fun_fierce_and_fantastical_african_art/transcript?language=en#t-229123

The Kennedy Center. (n.d.). Las Krudas. *The Kennedy Center: Las Krudas.* Retrieved February 23, 2022, from www.kennedy-center.org/artists/l/la-ln/-las-krudas/

Kim, J. B. (2017). Toward a Crip-of-Color Critique: Thinking with Minich's "Enabling Whom?" *Lateral, 6*(1). https://doi.org/10.25158/l6.1.14

Kozleski, E. B. (2010). Culturally Responsive Teaching Matters! *The Equity Alliance at ASU.* www.un.org/sustainabledevelopment/gender-equality/

Krudas Cubensi. (n.d.). *Krudas Cubensi.* Retrieved February 23, 2022, from https://krudascubensi.com/bio-press-krudas-cubensi/

Ladson-Billings, G. (2021). Three Decades of Culturally Relevant, Responsive, & Sustaining Pedagogy: What Lies Ahead? *The Educational Forum, 85*(4), 351–354. https://doi.org/10.1080/00131725.2021.1957632

Laughlin, K. A., Gallagher, J., Cobble, D. S., Boris, E., Nadasen, P., Gilmore, S., & Zarnow, L. (2010). Is It Time to Jump Ship? Historians Rethink the Waves Metaphor. *Feminist Formations*, 76–135.

Linderman, J. (2017, November 4). A Look at Women's Advances Over the Years in Congress. *PBS NewsHour*. Associated Press. https://www.pbs.org/new shour/politics/a-look-at-womens-advances-over-the-years-in-congress

Lorde, A. (2015). The Master's Tools Will Never Dismantle the Master's House. In C. Moraga & G. Anzaldúa's (Eds.), *This Bridge Called My Back: Writings by Radical Women of Color* (pp. 94–103). Suny Press.

Love, B. (2020). *We Want to Do More Than Survive: Abolitionist Teaching and the Pursuit of Educational Freedom* (Illustrated ed.). Beacon Press.

Made by Dyslexia. (2018, October 1). Dr Maggie Aderin-Pocock MBE: Made By Dyslexia Interview [Video]. *YouTube*. www.youtube.com/watch?v=xhJiC-ieXAg

Mancino, J. (2019, May 24). Meet the Kathoey: An Intro to Thailand's Unique Transgender Culture. *Jetset Times*. https://jetsettimes.com/lgbtq/meet-the-kathoey/

Martinez, C., & Carrington, K. (2021). Re-Thinking Gender, Artivism and Choices: Cultures of Equality Emerging from Urban Peripheries. *Frontiers in Sociology*, 6. https://doi.org/10.3389/fsoc.2021.637564

McCoy, T., & Traiano, H. (2020, November 15). He Grew Up White: Now He Identifies as Black: Brazil Grapples with Racial Redefinition. *Washington Post*. www.washingtonpost.com/world/the_americas/brazil-racial-identity-black-white/2020/11/15/2b7d41d2-21cb-11eb-8672-c281c7a2c96e_story.html

Michels, D. (2015). Sojourner Truth. *National Women's History Museum*. Retrieved November 10, 2021, from www.womenshistory.org/education-resources/biographies/sojourner-truth

Mitchell-Walthour, G. (2020, November 24). 'My Vote Will Be Black': A Wave of Afro-Brazilian Women Ran for Office in 2020 But Found Glass Ceiling Hard to Break. *The Conversation*. https://theconversation.com/my-vote-will-be-black-a-wave-of-afro-brazilian-women-ran-for-office-in-2020-but-found-glass-ceiling-hard-to-break-150521

Morris, M. (2018). *Pushout: The Criminalization of Black Girls in Schools* (First Trade Paper ed.). The New Press.

Museum of Contemporary Art San Diego. (2021). *Yolanda López: Portrait of the Artist*. Retrieved October 28, 2021, from www.mcasd.org/exhibitions/yolanda-l%C3%B3pez-portrait-artist

Nadkarni, A., & Subhalakshmi, G. (2017). Transnational Feminism. *Oxford Bibliographies Online in Literary and Critical Theory*. doi: 10.1093/obo/9780190221911-0006

National Abolition Hall of Fame and Museum. (n.d.). *Sojourner Truth*. Retrieved November 14, 2021, from www.nationalabolitionhalloffame-andmuseum.org/sojourner-truth.html

Ngomsi, V. (2021, June 30). *Annie Segarra*. https://invisibleproject.org/annie-segarra/

Norris, S. (2018, October 1). 'Anger Is Language of Justice' Says Author of New Book on Women's Rage. *Open Democracy*. www.opendemocracy.net/en/5050/anger-language-of-justice-new-book-womens-rage/

O'Keeffe, G. (n.d.). A Quote from Georgia O'Keeffe. *Goodreads*. Retrieved October 11, 2021, from www.goodreads.com/quotes/43946-nobody-sees-a-flower-really-it-is-so

Osborn, C. (2014, November 20). Black Brazilian Women Are Building Up Their Power: And They're Even Showing It with Their Hairstyle. *The World from PRX*. Retrieved December 17, 2021, from https://theworld.org/stories/2014-11-20/black-brazilian-women-are-finding-their-power-and-theyre-even-showing-it-their

Pattanaik, D. (2019, April 20). The Hijra Legacy. *Devdutt*. Retrieved March 23, 2022, from https://devdutt.com/articles/the-hijra-legacy/

Pavey, H. (2017, July 26). 35% of Women Cautioned for Their Appearance at Work Were Deemed "Distracting" to Their Male Counterparts. *Business Insider*. Retrieved January 9, 2022, from https://www.businessinsider.com/1-in-4-women-have-been-cautioned-about-their-appearance-in-workplace-2017-7?international=true&r=US&IR=T

PBS. (2021, November 23). Caretakers: Filipino Nurses and Care Workers in the United States—. *Chasing the Dream*. Retrieved February 20, 2022, from www.pbs.org/wnet/chasing-the-dream/series/caretakers/

Poetry Foundation. (2021). *Audre Lorde*. Retrieved October 10, 2021, from www.poetryfoundation.org/poets/audre-lorde

Pruitt-Young, S. (2021, August 6). Canadian Soccer Player Quinn Becomes the First Out Trans and Nonbinary Gold Medalist. *NPR*. Retrieved February 20, 2022, from www.npr.org/2021/08/06/1025442511/canadian-soccer-player-quinn-becomes-first-trans-and-nonbinary-olympic-gold-meda

Read Vice-President Elect Kamala Harris' Full Victory Speech. (2020, November 7). *PBS*. Retrieved November 4, 2021, from www.pbs.org/newshour/politics/read-vice-president-elect-kamala-harris-full-victory-speech

Rich, A. (2003). *What Is Found There: Notebooks on Poetry and Politics* (Expanded ed.). W. W. Norton & Company.

Rise Art. (2021, January 7). *A Guide to the Feminist Art Movement's History & Contemporary Impact*. www.riseart.com/guide/2418/guide-to-the-feminist-art-movement

Rivas, M. (February 2, 2022). Opal Lee Is Known as the 'Grandmother of Juneteenth'. Could 'Nobel Laureate' Be Next? *Fort Worth Star Telegram*. www.star-telegram.com/news/local/crossroads-lab/article257896338.html#storylink=cpy

Rocero, G. (2015, January 2). Model: Why I Came Out as Transgender. *CNN*. Retrieved February 20, 2022, from https://edition.cnn.com/2014/03/31/opinion/rocero-transgender-understanding/index.html

Rodriguez, L. (2020, September 21). 5 Laws Ruth Bader Ginsburg Championed to Support Gender Equality. *Global Citizen*. www.globalcitizen.org/en/content/gender-equality-laws-quotes-ruth-bader-ginsburg/

Rouvalis, C. (2022, February 16). A Representative Rep with a Determined "Boots-on-the-Ground Strategy." *Pittsburgh Magazine*. www.pittsburghmagazine.com/a-representative-rep-with-a-determined-boots-on-the-ground-strategy/

Roy, A. (2004). *An Ordinary Person's Guide to Empire* (1st ed.). South End Press.

Schalk, S., & Kim, J. B. (2020). Integrating Race, Transforming Feminist Disability Studies. *Signs: Journal of Women in Culture and Society*, 46(1), 31–55. https://doi.org/10.1086/709213

Scott, S. (2020, October 26). More Black Girl Magic! Brazil Crowned First Black Miss Brazil in 30 Years. *Essence*. www.essence.com/news/black-miss-brazil-crowned-raissa-santana/

Shamsia Hassani—Official Website. (2021). *Shamsia Hassani*. www.shamsia-hassani.net/

Simmons, D. (2012, August 29). Guest Blog: Emancipatory Education: Dena Simmons on Teaching for Social Justice in Middle School. *Feminist Teacher*. Retrieved December 10, 2021, from https://feministteacher.com/2012/08/29/guest-blog-emancipatory-education-dena-simmons-on-teaching-for-social-justice-in-middle-school/#more-1144

Simmons, D. (2021). Humanity, Healing and Doing the Work. *Learning for Justice*. Retrieved October 12, 2021, from www.learningforjustice.org/magazine/fall-2021/humanity-healing-and-doing-the-work

Tapp, T. (2021, August 27). Model, Writer, Director & Transgender Advocate Geena Rocero Signs with the Gotham Group. *Deadline*. Retrieved February 20, 2022, from https://deadline.com/2021/08/model-transgender-advocate-geena-rocero-gotham-group-1234823086/

Taylor, K. (2020, July 20). Until Black Women Are Free, None of Us Will Be Free. *The New Yorker*. www.newyorker.com/news/our-columnists/until-black-women-are-free-none-of-us-will-be-free

TBR Newsroom. (2019, December 5). The Face of Modern Slavery in Brazil. *The Brazilian Report*. Retrieved March 21, 2022, from https://brazilian.report/society/2019/11/28/precisao-documentary-face-modern-slavery-brazil/

Thompson, D. (2020). *Activist Annie Segarra Is on a Mission to Make Disabilities More Visible. In the Know.* www.intheknow.com/post/activist-annie-segarra-is-on-a-mission-to-make-disabilities-more-visible/

#Thosewhoinspireus: Emma Amos. (2020, July 12). *Alabama Chanin Journal.* https://journal.alabamachanin.com/2020/07/thosewhoinspireus-emma-amos

The Trevor Project. (n.d.). *The Trevor Project National Survey.* Retrieved February 20, 2022, from www.thetrevorproject.org/survey-2021/?section=Introduction

Truth, S. (1851). Ain't I a Woman? *Learning for Justice.* www.learningforjustice.org/classroom-resources/texts/aint-i-a-woman

Tuck, E. (2009). Suspending Damage: A Letter to Communities. *Harvard Educational Review, 79,* 409–428.

UN Foundation. (2015, March 3). Want to Change the World? Educate a Girl. *UN Foundation.* https://unfoundation.exposure.co/want-to-change-the-world-educate-a-girl

UNICEF. (n.d.). *Girls' Education.* https://www.unicef.org/education/girls-education

United Nations. (n.d.-a). *Goal 5: Achieve Gender Equality and Empower All Women and Girls.* https://www.un.org/sustainabledevelopment/gender-equality/

United Nations. (n.d.-b). Goal 5: Gender Equality: SDG Tracker. *Our World in Data.* Retrieved September 3, 2021, from https://sdg-tracker.org/gender-equality

United Nations. (n.d.-c). *Women's Job Market Participation Stagnating at Less Than 50% for the Past 25 Years, Finds UN Report.* https://www.un.org/en/desa/women%E2%80%99s-job-market-participation-stagnating-less-50-past-25-years-finds-un-report

United Nations. (2013, July 12). Malala Yousafzai Addresses United Nations Youth Assembly [Video]. *YouTube.* www.youtube.com/watch?v=3rN-hZu3ttIU

United Nations. (2014, September 22). Emma Watson at the HeForShe Campaign 2014: Official UN Video [Video]. *YouTube.* www.youtube.com/watch?v=gkjW9PZBRfk

United Nations. (2020). United Nations: Gender Equality and Women's Empowerment. *United Nations Sustainable Development.* Retrieved September 3, 2021, from www.un.org/sustainabledevelopment/gender-equality/

United Nations Department of Economic and Social Affairs. (2017). *World Day of Social Justice 2017 | DISD.* www.un.org/development/desa/dspd/international-days/world-day-of-social-justice/world-day-of-social-justice-2017.html

UN Women. (n.d.-a). *Equal Pay for Work of Equal Value*. UN Women. https://www.unwomen.org/en/news/in-focus/csw61/equal-pay

UN Women. (n.d.-b). *In Focus: UN Commission on the Status of Women (CSW65)*. UN Women. Retrieved July 26, 2022, from https://www.unwomen.org/en/news/in-focus/csw65

UN Women. (2020, July 1). *Intersectional Feminism: What It Means and Why It Matters Right Now*. www.unwomen.org/en/news/stories/2020/6/explainer-intersectional-feminism-what-it-means-and-why-it-matters

UN Women. (2021a, January 15). *Facts and Figures: Women's Leadership and Political Participation*. https://www.unwomen.org/en/what-we-do/leadership-and-political-participation/facts-and-figures

UN Women. (2021b, March 5). *Four Facts You Need to Know about Gender and Poverty Today*. UN Women. https://data.unwomen.org/features/four-facts-you-need-know-about-gender-and-poverty-today

UN Women. (2022, February). *Facts and Figures: Ending Violence against Women*. UN Women. https://www.unwomen.org/en/what-we-do/ending-violence-against-women/facts-and-figures

Wamsley, L. (2021, March 24). Rachel Levine Makes History As 1st Openly Trans Federal Official Confirmed By Senate. *NPR*. Retrieved February 20, 2022, from www.npr.org/2021/03/24/980788146/senate-confirms-rachel-levine-a-transgender-woman-as-assistant-health-secretary

Webteam. (2011, June 1). Carol Gillian. *Ethics of Care*. https://ethicsofcare.org/carol-gilligan/

The Women's Building. (2019, June 20). *Mission & History: The Women's Building*. Retrieved October 10, 2021, from https://womensbuilding.org/about/mission-history/

Woodson, M. (2020, October 6). Celebrating Beauty and Color: Mikela Henry-Lowe. *Artists Network*. www.artistsnetwork.com/art-mediums/color-portrait-painting-celebrating-beauty-mikela-henry-lowe/

The World. (2020, February 13). *Artist Christine Sun Kim on 'Deaf Rage,' the Super Bowl and the Power*. The World from PRX.

World Health Organization. (2021, November 24). Disability and Health. www.who.int/news-room/fact-sheets/detail/disability-and-health. Retrieved March 1, 2022, from www.who.int/news-room/fact-sheets/detail/disability-and-health

The Yale Center for Dyslexia and Creativity. (2014). Maggie Aderin-Pocock, Ph.D., Space Scientist & Science Communicator. *Yale Dyslexia*. https://dyslexia.yale.edu/story/maggie-aderin-pocock-ph-d/

Index

Taylor & Francis Group
an **informa** business

Taylor & Francis eBooks

www.taylorfrancis.com

A single destination for eBooks from Taylor & Francis
with increased functionality and an improved user
experience to meet the needs of our customers.

90,000+ eBooks of award-winning academic content in
Humanities, Social Science, Science, Technology, Engineering,
and Medical written by a global network of editors and authors.

TAYLOR & FRANCIS EBOOKS OFFERS:

A streamlined
experience for
our library
customers

A single point
of discovery
for all of our
eBook content

Improved
search and
discovery of
content at both
book and
chapter level

REQUEST A FREE TRIAL
support@taylorfrancis.com

 Routledge
Taylor & Francis Group

 CRC Press
Taylor & Francis Group

For Product Safety Concerns and Information please contact our EU
representative GPSR@taylorandfrancis.com
Taylor & Francis Verlag GmbH, Kaufingerstraße 24, 80331 München, Germany

www.ingramcontent.com/pod-product-compliance
Ingram Content Group UK Ltd.
Pitfield, Milton Keynes, MK11 3LW, UK
UKHW031041080625
459435UK00013B/566